The Legacy of
Buford Pusser

Turner Publishing Company
Paducah, Kentucky

Turner Publishing Company
412 Broadway, P.O. Box 3101
Paducah, Kentucky 42002-3101
(502) 443-0121

Copyright © 1994 W.R. Morris
All Rights Reserved

Publishing Consultant — Kenny R. Rose
Cover Design — Herbert C. Banks, II
Book Design — Luke A. Henry

This book or any part thereof may not be reproduced without the written consent of the author and publisher.

Library of Congress Catalog Card No. 94-61035
ISBN No. 1-56311-164-0

Printed in Tennessee.

Special Limited Edition.

Photo Credits: Cover photo by W.R. Morris. Most of the photographs in this publication were either taken by W.R. Morris, given to him by Buford or Helen Pusser, or provided by the person in the photo. Other credits are listed under the illustrations in the book.

The Legacy of Buford Pusser

A Pictorial History of the "Walking Tall" Sheriff

W.R. Morris

This book is dedicated to my daughter, Deborah Marie, and to my sons: David Lynn, Warren Robert, and Lance Jay Morris.

Introduction

Buford Pusser's name is etched in history. His narrow escapes from death, his brute force, his sometimes violent enforcement of law and order, his tireless crusade against moonshiners, and his war with the gang of thieves and murderers who ran the dives along the Tennessee-Mississippi state line drew much attention to the Tennessee sheriff.

W.R. Morris, a Tennessee-born writer, recorded the saga of the colorful and controversial lawman in a book entitled ***The Twelfth of August***. It sold over one million copies and inspired the "***Walking Tall***" movie series. After Pusser left office in 1970, he and Morris traveled the United States together to promote the book and the motion picture. The sheriff and the author became very close friends. Few persons knew Buford Pusser as well as W.R. Morris. Today, ***The Twelfth of August*** is still in much demand.

Buford, Morris's second book about Pusser, revealed another side of the legend. The books told the real stories that Bing Crosby Productions failed to present in their movies.

After meeting W.R. Morris for the first time in a small country grocery near Reagan, Tennessee, I purchased his latest book ***The State-Line Mob***. I was captivated by the details it contained. I learned who did what to whom, for how much money, why, and when. Such books make fascinating movies.

I visited with W.R. Morris on several occasions and saw the massive amount of Pusser material he had accumulated. Included were scores of photographs. Thus was born this pictorial history book about Buford Pusser and many of the events which helped to compose his legend. In this book, you will see many rare photos of Pusser, his family, and the incidents that shaped their lives. For the first time, you will see the never-before-published photos of Buford Pusser's face when it was ripped apart by high-powered rifle bullets in the ambush that killed his wife and left him near death.

Buford Pusser has been deceased for more than 20 years, but his legacy continues. He will be remembered as one of the tallest figures in the history of law enforcement.

— Kenny R. Rose

Acknowledgments

This is a work of nonfiction, based entirely on factual material, personal interviews, and years of research.

There are certain persons whose contributions to my work are special: Cathy Morris, my wife, who served as my trusted advisor and typed the manuscript; Maxene McDaniel; Kenny R. Rose; Steve Beal; Billy Wagoner; Rusty Larson; Peatie Plunk; Roger Aultman; and Howard Douglass.

— W.R. Morris

Other books by W. R. Morris

THE TWELFTH OF AUGUST

MEN BEHIND THE GUNS

ALIAS OSWALD

BUFORD

THE STATE-LINE MOB

W.R. MORRIS
P.O. BOX 63
REAGAN, TENNESSEE 38368

901-967-1341

Buford Pusser's winning bouts with death made him Tennessee's greatest hero since Davy Crockett. The legend, fed by raw violence, grew to giant stature during Pusser's short life.

Buford Pusser and I traveled the United States together to promote his authorized biography, The Twelfth of August, and the "Walking Tall" movie. Fortunately for us, the book became a best-seller and the movie a box-office smash.

When the 36-year-old Pusser died in a fiery car crash on August 21, 1974, he left behind a powerful legend. That legend is echoed in the pages of this book.

W. R. Morris

author of "Walking Tall" Sheriff Buford Pusser's best-selling biography, *The Twelfth of August*.

In memory of a close friend, **William Terry George**, *who was among Buford Pusser's greatest admirers. Although Terry, at age 33, lost a long battle with cancer, he always walked tall.*

The Legacy of Buford Pusser

Buford Pusser

Buford Pusser was an American folk hero. He cast across the nation one of the tallest shadows in law-enforcement history. His daring exploits as McNairy County, Tennessee, sheriff made him a legend in his own time.

Pusser was a rugged symbol of justice. He clawed his way to worldwide recognition. Shy and soft-spoken, he stood six-feet-six and weighed 250 pounds.

His war against crime bore a high price tag. Buford Pusser was shot eight times, stabbed seven, rammed with a moonshiner's car, and forced to kill two persons in the line of duty. Hand-to-hand combat with the outlaws left its battle scars on Pusser. His wire-meshed jaw, the gift of plastic surgeons, barely moved when he spoke.

Pusser underwent 16 facial operations following that tragic morning of August 12, 1967, when gangsters shot away the lower part of his face and murdered his wife in a predawn ambush intended for him. That was the day Buford Pusser served final notice on the mob that the South was not big enough for both of them.

Pusser eventually rose to national prominence through the pages of his biography, <u>The Twelfth of August</u>, and the "Walking Tall" movie.

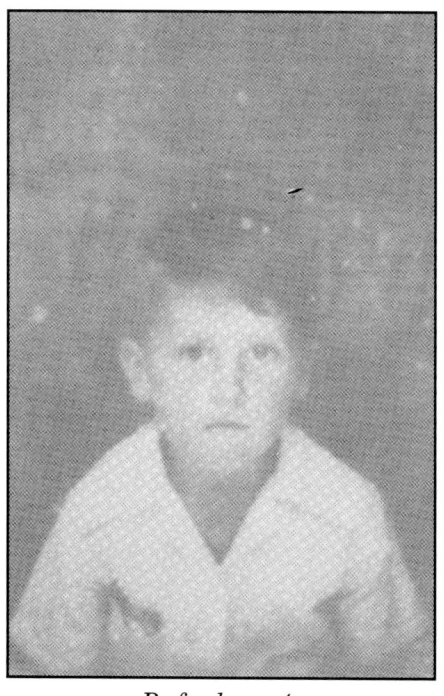
Buford age 4.

Buford Hayse Pusser was born December 12, 1937, in a weather-beaten farmhouse near Finger, Tennessee. He weighed nine pounds, six ounces. He was the third child of Carl and Helen Pusser with John Howard being the oldest offspring and Gailya the only girl.

The Pussers barely scratched out a living in the McNairy County cotton fields. West Tennessee was still feeling the pinch of the Depression, and even money for necessities was almost nonexistent. Between crops, Carl Pusser, a big, muscular man, labored at a sawmill for 50¢ a day. He also became a self-made barber, cutting hair on Sundays for a nickel a head.

Buford Pusser grew into a timid, almost backward boy. During his early childhood, he clung tightly to his mother's apron strings. When Buford was not under Helen Pusser's wing, he felt crippled.

The mother-son weld created a major problem when first-grade registration rolled around. Buford refused to enter classes at Finger School. "I don't want to go to school till I'm 40 years old!" he told his mother.

Although Helen Pusser thought her son's remarks were amusing, she was determined to enroll him. Buford protested and begged his mother to let him stay home from school. When she forced him to go, he cried.

Once he was finally pushed away from his mother's shadow, Pusser found a hostile world among the other youngsters at Finger Elementary. Because he was shy, he became the object of much laughter. The older boys teased him, and when he refused to fight back, the taunting grew steadily worse.

Buford continued to plead with his mother to take him out of school. She tolerated his tantrums for two months, then made a bargain with him. He could remain home until the next school year; then he would have to go. Regardless.

Buford age 6.

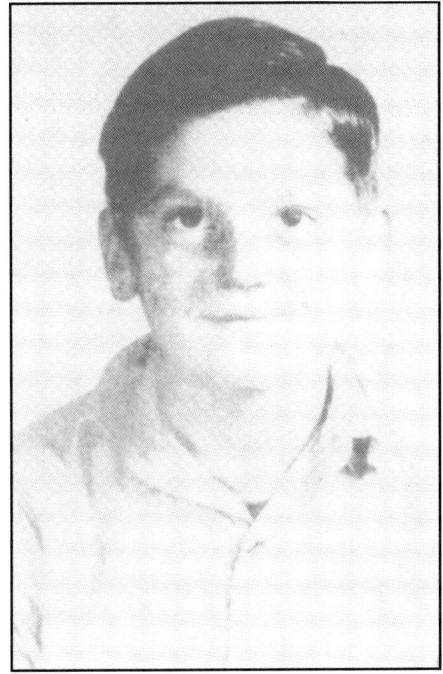
Buford age 8.

The following school term, Mrs. Pusser, using a little more muscle than usual, forced Buford to enter the first grade at Leapwood School. She hoped a new school environment might soften his rebellious attitude. With constant pressure from his mother, Buford remained there through the fifth grade.

The next autumn, Helen Pusser registered Buford in the sixth grade at Adamsville Elementary. He rode the school bus to and from Adamsville on weekdays but would not ride it to special school functions. Still timid and shy at age 11, he was afraid he would get lost if he rode the bus anywhere except back and forth to school.

John Howard, Buford (one year old), and Gailya on the Pusser farm near Finger, Tennessee, in 1938.

Carl and Helen Pusser in 1977. Carl died in January 1978.

THE LEGACY OF BUFORD PUSSER

Buford Pusser, barely ten months old, is held by his sister, Gailya, in a cane-bottom chair on the Pusser farm near Finger.

The Pusser family in 1966. From left to right: Buford, Gailya, Helen, John Howard, and Carl. Buford's sister, Gailya Davis, is the only surviving member.

17

For a time, Buford remained close to his mother. But in 1950, he loosened the reins enough to hire out for his first job. Charlie Duren, owner of a general store in Adamsville, employed Buford to mow his lawn, trim hedges around his house, and plow and plant his garden.

In 1951, Carl Pusser decided it was time to give up trying to support the family from his barely productive farm. He found employment with a construction cleanup crew in Columbia, Tennessee. Buford's older siblings, John Howard and Gailya, had already left home in search of greener pastures. Carl's departure left Buford and Helen with the task of making a crop. Although he was only 13 years old, Buford readily accepted the challenge.

By the end of the harvest season, young Pusser had learned that he could successfully do his father's work on the farm, thus proving to himself that he could shoulder a man's responsibility. He attended eighth-grade classes at Adamsville Elementary and worked after school and on Saturdays at Duren's store. His job now included the loading and delivering of feed and supplies to farmers.

Early in 1952, the Pussers moved from the farm at Finger to a small frame house in Adamsville. Carl was working steadily with a construction company that had commitments to lay pipelines in Mississippi and Louisiana. Buford was elated. He said farewell to planting crops, worrying about rain, and keeping tabs on the cotton market.

Buford Pusser, after much prodding from his mother, graduated from Adamsville Elementary School. He disliked attending classes during his early childhood years.

Buford Pusser at age 16.

Buford Pusser atop a Civil War cannon in 1955 at the Shiloh National Military Park in Shiloh, Tennessee.

THE LEGACY OF BUFORD PUSSER

Meanwhile, Buford Pusser did manage to maintain average grades in school, and he graduated from Adamsville Elementary. Immediately following that milestone, he went to work full-time at Duren's store for the summer.

In the fall, Pusser entered Adamsville High School. Right away, he took an interest in athletics, and Coach Max Hile named him the starting fullback for the Adamsville Cardinals. The hard-charging Pusser kept local fans talking about his fakes and his broken field running. When the football season ended, no one, especially Cardinal opponents, doubted Buford's ability to play football.

T. E. Chism, the Redbird basketball coach, was also impressed with Pusser's athletic talents. He made Buford a starting guard, and the tall freshman led the team with a 27-point average.

Buford Pusser in high school.

Sports made the first two years of high school more tolerable for Pusser, but early in his junior year, he ran into trouble with his studies. Failing two subjects (history and biology), he dropped out of school. Although disappointed, Helen Pusser gave Buford permission to work on a pipeline in Wynnewood, Oklahoma.

After six weeks, Mrs. Pusser was thoroughly discontented. She implored her youngest child to come home and finish high school. A patient woman with a will of iron, Helen Pusser borrowed history and biology textbooks from the school library and studied so that she would be able to tutor Buford. When Pusser learned what his mother was doing, he quit his pipeline job and returned to Adamsville.

With Helen Pusser's help, Buford managed to make up the time he had lost and his failing grades. He studied diligently after returning to his junior class, determined to repay his mother for all she had done to get him back in school.

For a while, Pusser spent every night with his nose in his schoolbooks, but eventually a hunger for excitement weakened him. One December evening in 1954, just before his 17th birthday, he got his first taste of the state-line activities.

Pusser and two of his buddies watched Louise Hathcock, owner of the White Iris Club, beat a sailor to death with a claw hammer. The state-line madam told a deputy sheriff that the sailor had apparently died of a heart attack.

THE LEGACY OF BUFORD PUSSER

"All right, Louise, if you say so," the lawman grinned. "Get me a drink while I call an ambulance."

Buford Pusser had gotten his first look at Louise Hathcock. In later years, their paths would cross again, but Pusser would never forget his first visit to the White Iris.

Louise Anderson, born March 19, 1919, in West Point, Mississippi, had come to Alcorn County in hopes of crawling from poverty. Flat broke when she arrived in mid-1937, the teenager sauntered into luck. She met a young hoodlum who had more money than he had brains.

Jack Hathcock, barely old enough to shave, was managing the State-Line Club, a crude, off-white block building that straddled the border. L. A. "Kay" Timlake, a wealthy Corinth jukebox operator, owned the honky-tonk. With Jack's better than average paycheck, along with the money he swiped from the cash register, he was rolling in dough.

Louise Anderson's good looks immediately caught Hathcock in a love trap, and his wad of greenbacks temporarily stunned her.

On October 3, 1937, Louise married Jack Hathcock in Corinth. Both lied about their ages on the marriage license application. Louise, who was 18, claimed that she was a year older, and Jack, who was only 17, swore that he was 21.

Buford Pusser, 18, and his girlfriend Norma Jean Gilchrist in 1955. Pusser dated Miss Gilchrist after he returned home from an Oklahoma pipeline job and reentered classes at Adamsville High School.

Jack Hathcock and his gang corrupted the state line long before Buford Pusser became sheriff of McNairy County. The Forty-Five Grill, which opened in 1950, was a den of crooked card games, bootlegging, prostitution, and rigged dice tables.

THE LEGACY OF BUFORD PUSSER

Alcorn County Sheriff Lyle Taylor and his deputies inventory a cache of bootleg whiskey during a raid of the Forty-Five Grill in 1956. From left to right are Taylor, Earl Mills, R.C. McNair, and Grady Bingham. Bingham later served as sheriff of Alcorn County during the time Buford Pusser was McNairy County's top lawman.

Buford's graduation.

Jack Hathcock, who became an outlaw in his early teens, organized the state-line mob along the Tennessee-Mississippi border. Photo copyrighted by W.R. Morris

Actually, Louise had no desire to spend the rest of her life with Jack Hathcock. But neither did she want to spend the rest of her life wondering where she would get her next meal.

Poverty had scarred and molded Jack Hathcock at an early age. His parents had labored in the cotton fields to rear Jack and his five sisters and four brothers.

The Hathcock farm, less than forty acres, was near Michie, a tiny settlement in southeastern McNairy County.

Jack picked up spending money by bootlegging moonshine whiskey. He peddled the booze from saddlebags on the white horse he rode to the Michie Elementary School. He rarely attended classes but usually sold the liquor to his young "clients" on the school yard and left.

Born Clyde Raymond Hathcock on July 26, 1920, in Michie, he was known to everyone, for some unexplained reason, as "Jack."

He was tall and slender with a full head of dark brown hair and was almost illiterate. From birth, his speech had been flawed by an impediment that had gradually improved with age.

Timlake hired the 16-year-old Hathcock fresh from the Tennessee Reformatory in Nashville, where he had been locked up for pilfering houses in McNairy County.

With the help of his mother, Buford Pusser squeezed through high school, and in the spring of 1956, he received his diploma.

After graduation, Pusser found himself all grown up and feeling restless. He wanted to see the world, and he knew exactly how to accomplish that goal. On August 9, 1956, Buford Pusser joined the U.S. Marines and journeyed to Parris Island, South Carolina, for basic training.

Less than a month after Pusser's arrival at

the training camp, military doctors discovered that he had asthma. He was sent to the naval hospital at Beaufort, South Carolina, and on November 14, 1956, the Marines handed him a medical discharge.

Meanwhile, Carl Pusser had quit his construction job, and the Adamsville City Board had named him police chief.

Buford Pusser's venture into the outside world had been cut short too soon. He was restless and moody. It had been several weeks since he had seen his sister, Gailya, who lived in Memphis. Pusser asked Billy Earl Christopher, a close friend, to drive him to the Bluff City on November 25.

That night, as the young men made their way back home to Adamsville, Buford Pusser had his first brush with death. Christopher was forced off

Pusser in the Marines.

the road by another vehicle, and his car crashed into a side ditch. Pusser was thrown from the automobile. Suffering a broken back, he was rushed to the Baptist Hospital in Memphis. With his 19th birthday less than three weeks away, he was overwhelmed with a fear of death. But that experience was just the beginning. The shadow of death would stalk Buford Pusser for the rest of his life.

On January 4, 1957, Pusser was discharged from the hospital. He recuperated at his parents' house.

Trapped by inactivity and boredom, Buford Pusser decided to make another trip to the state line. Near the end of February, he drove his old Chevrolet to the Plantation Club. The dive, owned by W. O. Hathcock, Jr., was located beside U.S. 45, just inside the Mississippi line. Pusser still had about $75 of his mustering-out pay from the Marines. He decided to try his hand at dice. His luck was good.

With Pusser's dice-table winnings, he had about $200 in his pocket when four husky men grabbed him. They beat the young ex-Marine to the floor, then kicked him repeatedly in the face with sharp-toed boots. After pilfering Pusser's pockets, the thugs threw him out the back door. As he lay sprawled facedown in the gravel and a slowly falling rain, Buford Pusser swore to get even with the state-line mob someday.

Pusser drove himself to the Humphrey-Phillips Clinic in Selmer. It took 192 stitches to close the wounds in his head and face.

Early in April 1957, Marvin Hailey, manager of the Shackelford Funeral Home in Selmer, hired Buford Pusser to drive an ambulance and help with funerals. The pay was $160 a month plus a commission for each funeral.

Pusser enjoyed the work – driving ambulances, serving as a part-time pallbearer, comforting grief-stricken families and friends, and performing all the other chores that went with the job. But Pusser was not satisfied with the pay. He had expected the commissions to be much higher.

Other McNairy County boys had gone to Chicago after school and often returned home to visit, bragging about their hefty paychecks.

Late in August, Buford Pusser turned in the keys to his Shackelford ambulance, drew his final pay, and headed for the Windy City. Pusser took a job as a die-cutting machine operator at the Union Bag Company. He was pleased with his new salary and felt encouraged.

For some strange reason, Pusser had always been intrigued by death. In an effort to better understand his fascination, he enrolled in Worsham's College, a morticians' school. Eventually the strain of attending classes and keeping up with his studies while working a full shift at the mill became too much. After nine months of study, Pusser left Worsham's.

Buford Pusser and Pauline Mullins Vance were married on December 5, 1959, in Chicago, Illinois.

Wrestler Buford Pusser.

In 1958, Pusser found a new way to earn extra money and, at the same time, keep himself in top physical shape. He began wrestling professionally on weekends. A tall, muscular specimen, he was a natural crowd pleaser.

One night in Chicago, as Pusser strolled from his dressing room, he met a blond divorcee from Haysi, Virginia. Her name was Pauline Mullins Vance. She and Pusser quickly became friends. Buford spent much time with Pauline and her two small children, Diane and Mike.

Cupid worked rapidly. On December 5, 1959, Buford Pusser and Pauline Vance were married in a quiet ceremony before a justice of the peace in Chicago. The wedding took place just seven days before Buford's 22nd birthday. Pauline was three years older than her new husband.

Pusser adjusted quickly to married life. He now had a family to come home to, and his small apartment seemed a long, long way from the Tennessee-Mississippi state line.

Less than a month after his marriage, however, Pusser was arrested in Chicago on a warrant from Alcorn County, Mississippi. He was charged with armed robbery and attempted murder. According to the warrant, Pusser and two of his friends, Jerry Wright and Marvin King, Jr., had beaten and robbed W. O. Hathcock, Jr., at the Plantation Club on De-

Diane Vance.

Dwana Pusser at age 12.

Buford Pusser had two stepchildren and one natural child. From left to right: stepdaughter Diane Vance, daughter Dwana, and stepson Mike Vance.

 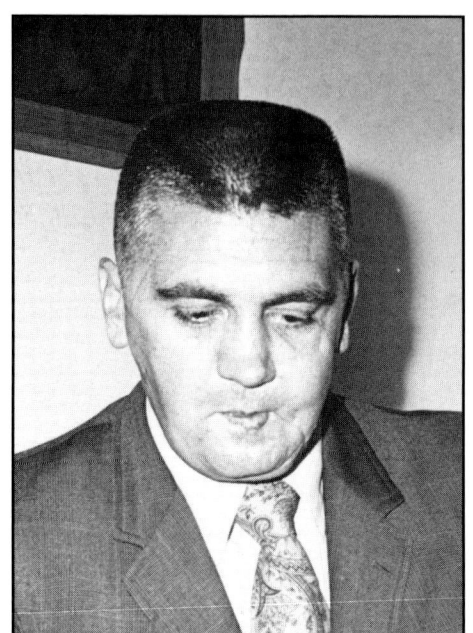

Pauline Pusser in 1966.   *Buford Pusser.*

cember 13, 1959. Hathcock claimed the three men had taken $1,176 from him at gunpoint, then pistol-whipped him, making it necessary for him to spend two weeks in the Corinth hospital.

During the trial, District Attorney N. S. "Soggy" Sweat contended that Pusser had recruited Wright and King to help him even the score with W. O. Hathcock. Sweat argued that Buford Pusser wanted revenge because Hathcock and his gang had beaten and robbed Pusser back in 1957.

Cary Stovall, defense attorney, quickly blew that theory out of the water. He produced official time cards from the Union Bag Company indicating that Pusser, Wright, and King were at work in Chicago when the crime occurred on December 12, 1959. The jury acquitted the three men.

After the trial, Buford Pusser's morale reached a low point. Things were going poorly on the job. Each day seemed like a month.

Pauline Pusser boosted her husband's spirits one evening when she informed him that he was going to be a father. Buford embraced his wife and kissed her repeatedly.

On January 9, 1961, Pauline Pusser gave birth to a nine-pound, four-ounce girl in Chicago's Ravenswood Hospital. The baby was named Dwana Aitoya Pusser.

For another year, Pusser worked at the paper mill, scuffled with sweating bodies on a canvas, and enjoyed his family when time permitted.

THE LEGACY OF BUFORD PUSSER

Early in 1962, Buford Pusser realized that whatever he was seeking was not to be found in Chicago. Pauline was not surprised when Buford told her he wanted to go home to McNairy County.

The Pussers moved into a rented house trailer in Adamsville, and Pauline enrolled Mike and Diane in the same elementary school that Buford had attended.

After a couple of weeks of unsuccessful job hunting, Pusser decided to start wrestling again. Although the skirmishes on canvas would not make him wealthy, Buford felt they would provide enough money to keep the creditors satisfied until he could obtain full-time employment.

Bouts were staged in many West Tennessee towns, and Buford

The Alcorn County Courthouse in Corinth, Mississippi, was the scene of Buford Pusser's 1960 armed robbery trial. Pusser and two of his friends were aquitted of robbing W.O. Hathcock, Jr., at the Plantation Club. Charges of assault with intent to commit murder that had been lodged against the three men were dropped.

Pusser's name soon became a household word in Southern wrestling circles. His fans came to believe he could whip any man single-handedly and often said, "Buford Pusser's not scared of the devil himself."

One Saturday afternoon, a circus promoter set up a ring in Savannah, Tennessee, and offered a $50 bill to anyone who could pin a 160-pound black bear to the mat. Buford Pusser knocked the muzzled bear to the canvas with a football block, then jumped on top of his furry opponent and pinned the animal to the tarp-covered floor.

The bear's owner attempted to weasel out of paying Pusser. When the professional wrestler demanded his 50 bucks or a pound of flesh, the promoter quickly paid Buford the cash. After all, who wanted to tangle with a man who had just floored a bear?

Three days later, Carl Pusser told Buford that he intended to resign from his police chief job. Carl Pusser had been walking with a limp and complaining of severe leg pains ever since October 1957, when a car ran his pickup truck off a backwoods road. The truck had turned over, pinning Pusser inside. Carl offered to help Buford replace him as chief of police. "If you want the position, son, I'll recommend that Mayor Blanton and the city board members hire you."

"I would really appreciate the job. I'd like to be in law enforcement," Buford replied.

Mayor Leonard Blanton called the three-man Adamsville city council together for a special meeting. The other two members were J. D. Abernathy and George Tidwell. Blanton got right down to business and suggested that the board hire Buford Pusser as the town's police chief. "I think Buford will make us a fine chief," Blanton said. "He is real polite, and he's big enough to gain the respect of everyone, including our young people. I highly recommend that we hire him."

The vote to employ Buford Pusser was unanimous.

Since Pusser was only 24 himself, he had little difficulty making friends with the local teenagers. When the youngsters sped through town, he stopped them and, in most cases, handed out warnings instead of tickets.

For those who seemed to be overwhelmed by an urge for fast

driving, Pusser worked out a special plan. Late at night, after the streets had cleared and the "old-fashioned" folks had climbed under the covers, Buford took the racing enthusiasts out to a deserted country road. He blocked it off, then turned the drag racers loose. Pusser always made the rules himself and personally supervised the events.

A crucial rule for the private racing club was never breaking the speed limit on any public street or highway. Those who were caught speeding would lose their "membership" in the special late-night club.

The teenagers grew to admire and respect Buford Pusser. They considered him one of their own.

In September 1962, Pusser decided to seek his first elected office, constable in the Third Civil District. Being a constable was only a part-time job, and if Buford won, it would not interfere with his chief of police work. Pusser defeated his opponent Tommy Morris, who had held the constable seat for several years, by more than 115 votes.

Pusser's goal, however, was to eventually become sheriff of McNairy County. Still thirsty for revenge because of his own unfortunate tangles with the Hathcocks and their state-line mob, Pusser wanted to rid the strip of criminal activity. And he wanted to do it legally – with the endorsement of law and order.

Early in 1964, Carl Pusser became Buford's campaign manager, and he began to solicit funds and votes. Campaigning day and night in all corners of McNairy County, Buford Pusser sought to reach as many of the 18,085 residents as possible. Running on the Republican ticket, he even went into traditionally Democratic communities. He was determined to change the voting trend.

As the pace of the campaign quickened, Buford Pusser's popularity increased. Talk that he would be the next sheriff circulated in the county. Many pledged to support him.

Buford, however, did not take the pledges too seriously. Talk was one thing, but going to the polls was

---

ELECT

BUFORD PUSSER

SHERIFF OF
McNAIRY COUNTY

Your Support Will Be Deeply Appreciated.

Pd. Pol. Adv. By Buford Pusser.

something else. He remembered the fate of Grand Ole Opry star Roy Acuff, also a Republican, who had lost his bid for governor a few years before. Acuff had a half-million Tennessee fans at the time, but when it came right down to it, only a few voted for him.

Louise Hathcock had also heard the rumors of a Pusser victory and hastened to send word to Buford that she had a $600 campaign gift for him. All he had to do was stop by the Shamrock Motel and pick it up.

Pusser scoffed at her offer. He hated Louise Hathcock and everything for which she stood. Her latest exploit had been the killing of her husband, Jack, on May 22, 1964. A McNairy County grand jury had no-billed her after she claimed, "It was him or me." Pusser was convinced that Louise had murdered Jack Hathcock simply to get him out of her way. Pusser would later learn that Carl Douglas "Towhead" White, Louise Hathcock's lover, had been the actual triggerman.

The campaign went smoothly until two weeks before the August election date. Sheriff James Dickey, barely 40 years old, was found dead in his wrecked car beside U.S. 45 Highway near the state line. Many people believed that Dickey had met death at the hands of the state-line mob. However, nothing to substantiate foul play was ever uncovered by county and state officials during an investigation of the car crash.

The three-way sheriff's race went down to the wire with Buford Pusser, Republican, beating independent candidate George Weatherford 3,288 to 3,040. In spite of Dickey's death, 307 Democrats cast ballots for him.

On September 1, 1964, Buford Pusser took his oath of office in McNairy County. At age 26, he became Tennessee's youngest sheriff.

Because he believed that he was physically capable of taking care of himself, Pusser decided that it would not be necessary for him to wear a pistol. He did, however, keep a hand weapon and a shotgun in his car.

For official patrol duties, the new sheriff purchased a 1965 Dodge Charger.

Buford hired his father, Carl, as a deputy and jailer. Carl's primary job would be to take care of the jail.

Pusser began making routine checks of the roadhouses and state-line joints on a regular basis. The White Iris, operated by Carl

The Shamrock Motel and Restaurant opened for business in June 1957. Authorities said that Jack and Louise Hathcock fleeced tourists out of more than $7,000 a week at the Shamrock. Some of the patrons ended up in the nearby Tennessee River.

Douglas "Towhead" White (an ex-convict who had vowed to become the Al Capone of the South), and the Shamrock Motel, owned and managed by Louise Hathcock, created the most problems for Pusser. The White Iris featured dancing, gambling, bootleg whiskey, and beer drinking. The main attractions at the Shamrock were prostitutes, con games, illegal whiskey and beer, and a special rate for one hour's use of a room.

Pusser kept an especially steady rein on the White Iris. Towhead White called it harassment. Buford called it doing his job.

White had arrived in Alcorn County with another outlaw named

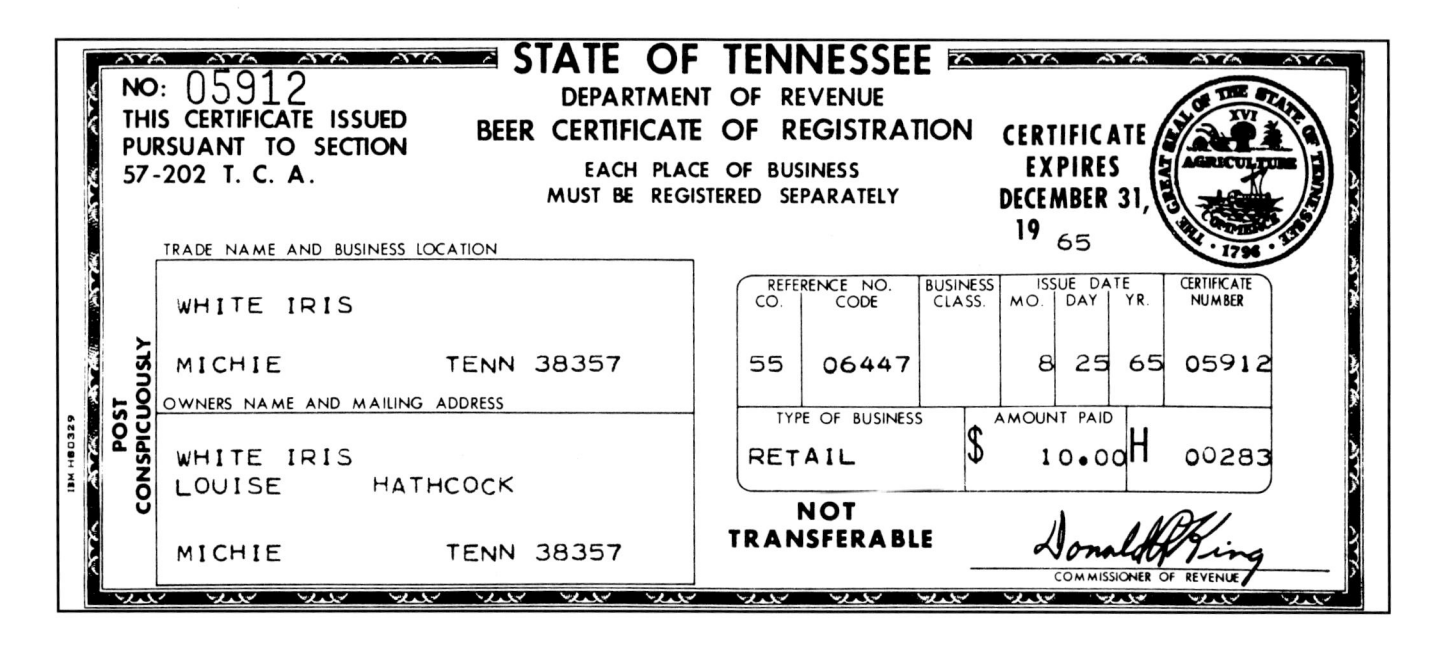

The White Iris was a trouble spot for Buford Pusser during his three terms as McNairy County sheriff. Louise Hathcock first operated the joint herself, then turned it over to her boyfriend Towhead White.

Berry "Junior" Smith in 1953. Born December 31, 1936, in the Friendship community near Sumner, Mississippi, Towhead White had been crossways with the law ever since he was 14 years old.

Although White often got into trouble, he had a knack for talking his way out of it. He had a smooth tongue and likable ways. His slender six-foot-two frame, soft brown eyes, innocent grin, and low, earnest voice worked to his advantage with women and with other men. He could laugh and joke one minute and then, with only his eyes showing the change, turn to solid granite the next. People

Carl Pusser during the time he was keeper of the McNairy County Jail.

Jack and Louise Hathcock spent little time together in this house on Proper Street in Corinth, Mississippi. Most of their time was consumed by illegal activities at the Shamrock Motel and Restaurant on the state line.

```
62-6010454 W
69-0630419
Town of Adamsville
Adamsville, Tennessee
```

WITHHOLDING TAX STATEMENT 1964
Federal taxes withheld from wages

Type or print EMPLOYER'S identification number, name, and address above.

Copy C—For employee's records

SOCIAL SECURITY INFORMATION		INCOME TAX INFORMATION	
$ 67.28 F.I.C.A. employee tax withheld, if any	$ 1,856.25 Total F.I.C.A. wages paid in 1964	$ 0 Federal income tax withheld, if any	$ 1,856.25 Total wages* paid in 1964

```
Buford Pusser
Adamsville, Tennessee

409-56-5267
```

NOTICE: If your wages were subject to social security taxes, but are not shown, your social security wages are the same as wages shown under "Income Tax Information," but not more than $4,800.
Keep this copy as part of your tax records.

Type or print EMPLOYEE'S social security account no., name, and address above.

FORM W-2—U.S. Treasury Department, Internal Revenue Service   *Before payroll deductions or "sick pay" exclusion.

```
County of McNairy
Howard Moore, Judge   62-6000755
Selmer, Tenn
```

WITHHOLDING TAX STATEMENT 1964
Federal taxes withheld from wages

Type or print EMPLOYER'S identification number, name, and address above.

Copy C—For employee's records

SOCIAL SECURITY INFORMATION		INCOME TAX INFORMATION	
$ 58.04 F.I.C.A. employee tax withheld, if any	$ 1,200.00 Total F.I.C.A. wages paid in 1964	$ 43.60 Federal income tax withheld, if any	$ 1,200.00 Total wages* paid in 1964

```
Buford Pusser
Selmer, Tenn.     409-56-5267
```

NOTICE: If your wages were subject to social security taxes, but are not shown, your social security wages are the same as wages shown under "Income Tax Information," but not more than $4,800.
Keep this copy as part of your tax records.

Type or print EMPLOYEE'S social security account no., name, and address above.

FORM W-2—U.S. Treasury Department, Internal Revenue Service   *Before payroll deductions or "sick pay" exclusion.

Buford Pusser's 1964 withholding tax statement for his Adamsville Police Chief job (top) and his first accounting of wages as sheriff of McNairy County. He earned $1,856.25 ($232.03 a month) from January to the end of August for being police chief, and the county paid him $1,200.00 ($300 per month) for wearing the sheriff's badge from September through December. The IRS gave him a $43.60 refund that year.

Buford Pusser strolls toward the McNairy County Courthouse shortly after taking over the sheriff's office on September 1, 1964.

HURST REELECTED

McNairy C[ounty]

VOLUME 63   SELMER, T[ENN.]

Watson in Road

From the Publisher's
Notebook
BY GEORGE HAMILTON

Do not put your wishbone where your backbone ought to be.

Lawzy mercy! Did you see what we pulled last week! Ran Bro. Owen Freeman's picture (he's to hold the meeting at Fourth Street Church of Christ) instead of Bro. Jimmy Stroud (he's to hold the meeting at Finger Baptist Church). We told Bro. Alfred Reeves, minister of the Fourth Street Church, though that we'd try to make amends by urging all to attend both meetings. The Fourth Street meeting is Aug. 24-30 with services at 10:30 a.m. and 7:30 p.m. The Finger Baptist meeting was postponed (notice elsewhere in the paper), with services at 7:30. Guess they'll both be glad to have you.

Our good friend, Herbert Morris, Sr., of Memphis will never know what he's missing until he moves to the country. F'rinstance, there was that lug of the most gorgeous, luscious-looking peaches we ever saw brought in and presented by Vance Wilson last week. They are so good they're simply too good to can, make into jam or what have you. Peaches of that

Junior Golf Winners

Present at the awarding of trophies for the fifth annual Jaycees junior golf tournament were, left to right: Maurice R. Hamm, Ray Hamm, Bill Abernathy, winner of second...

Hospital

Elected new officers of [hos]pital medical staff at the right: T. N. Humphrey, M.D., secretary; Monti[e]

THE LEGACY OF BUFORD PUSSER

PUSSER WINNER

nty Independent

FRIDAY, AUGUST 7, 1964   NUMBER 8

Post; Christopher Wins

Officers

Smith Elected School Board Member; Rogers, Hawkins Are Constables

An estimated crowd of more than 3,000 gathered in Selmer's court square Thursday night with interest high in the county's four hotly contested races for superintendent of education, sheriff, road commissioner and tax assessor.

With all returns in, Julius S. Hurst, the incumbent, had won an endorsement term, defeating his opponent, T. V. Jordan, principal of Adamsville High School, by a comfortable margin, 3988 to 2927.

W. Orlan Watson, who ran the incumbent, Ben Hockaday, a close race for road commissioner two years ago, was winner by a landslide with the vote showing

Capital Outlay Funds Mailed to

*This August 7, 1964, edition of the **McNairy County Independent** declares Julius Hurst the victor in the race for school superintendent and Buford Pusser winner of the sheriff's office.*

SHERIFF McNAIRY COUNTY

BUFORD PUSSER
SELMER, TENN. 38375

OFFICE: (901) 645-3406
RESIDENCE: 632-6190

This ticket for inmate groceries from Lewis Food Store was signed by Pauline Pusser.

This ticket for inmate groceries at the McNairy County Jail was signed by Carl Pusser.

did just about anything he asked of them. Those who knew him best said he could have become anything he wanted to be. What Carl Douglas "Towhead" White wanted to be, apparently, was one of the top hoods in the United States.

White decided to try a scare tactic on the new McNairy County sheriff by making some threatening telephone calls to Pusser's office in Selmer and his home in Adamsville. The first call was to Buford's office. Carl Pusser answered the phone.

"Listen, you old gray-headed scum bag, and listen good. There's a $10,000 reward on Buford's head, and I'm gonna collect it."

"Go ahead and collect it if you think yore man enough," Carl Pusser replied angrily, slamming down the telephone receiver.

The second call went to Buford's house. "We're gonna take your kids out in the swamp and cut off their sweet little heads. That way, the swamp water will get some colorin'," White told Pauline Pusser.

When the sheriff arrived home, he found his wife almost hysterical. Although he was angered by the call, Pusser forced himself to remain calm. He did not want to cause Pauline to be any more upset than she already was.

Buford Pusser knew that Towhead White was behind the telephone calls. One of the gangster's so-called friends, who was trying to butter up the sheriff, had tipped him.

Late one evening, as Towhead White sauntered from the White Iris Club and crossed U.S. 45 toward the Shamrock Motel, Buford Pusser braked his Dodge between the outlaw and the motor inn. Pusser had been watching the White Iris for more than an hour. "Get up against the car, White, and put your hands on top," Buford ordered, holding a .41-caliber magnum in his right hand.

"What's the idea, Pusser? You ain't got no right to do this!"

"Shut your mouth, and do as you're told before you get your head blown off!" The sheriff searched White and found a .38-caliber

Carl Douglas "Towhead" White, vowing to be the Al Capone of the South, arrived in Alcorn County, Mississippi, in 1953. He later became boss of the state-line mob. Photo copyrighted by W.R. Morris

Tommy Bivens and Towhead White were "old friends" until the gangster tried to kill Bivens at the Shamrock Restaurant on June 20, 1964. Bivens, a dragline operator, was a regular at the state-line joints. Unlike most of his buddies at the border, Bivens did not participate in robberies and murders. Until recently, he owned a nightclub near the state line.

Ron Windsor, wild and reckless during his youth, was a close friend of Towhead White. Windsor later became a lawyer and prosecuting attorney of Alcorn County, Mississippi.

pistol in a shoulder holster under his expensive suit coat. "This kind of hardware is illegal. But I'm sure a good, law-abidin' citizen like you didn't know that," Pusser snapped as he slipped the weapon into his own jacket pocket. Pusser handcuffed the gangster, then ordered him into the front seat of the car.

"You ain't got no right to kidnap me like this," protested White.

"I'm not kidnappin' you. I found a pistol on you, and I'm holdin' you for investigation."

"Investigation of what?"

"Murder, threatenin' telephone calls, robbery. Just name it; you've done it," growled Pusser.

"You ain't got a thing on me, Pusser! And you know it!"

"Tell me another joke. You called my wife and threatened her with a lotta nasty things. You also called my father. Now you're gonna pay for those calls."

Towhead White denied the allegations. Always before, he had been able to talk his way out of trouble. But not this time.

Pusser whipped his Dodge onto a gravel road which led to the Hatchie River. The car lights shimmered off the murky waters. The entire area was swampy; and when the river overflowed, stagnant water stood for weeks in the bottomlands. On that particular night, the river was out of its banks.

Pusser stopped the car. "Get out, White!"

"Look, sheriff. You're a man of the law. You're supposed to protect me, not murder me."

"That's a laugh. A cold-blooded killer like you talkin' about protection of the law. Now get out before I drag you out!"

White slid from the seat and stood beside the

car. He knew Pusser was almost insane with anger. For the first time in his criminal career, Carl Douglas "Towhead" White was frightened.

Buford Pusser slammed his fist into the hoodlum's face. White staggered back a couple of steps. The sheriff quickly followed with another punch that caught his victim in the mouth. The state-line thug fell into the soft mud near the edge of the water. Pusser kicked him hard in the jaw. Blood streaked White's face. Buford cocked the magnum. "Crawl! Crawl until the elbows and knees are out of that 200-dollar Italian suit and those 50-dollar Stacy shoes are ruined!"

It was difficult for White to move with his hands shackled, but he managed.

"I'm gonna kill you, Towhead, then throw you in the river weighted down with iron and chains. You know, the way you and Louise and the other state-line goons do it with all those people you shoot and rob."

White struggled to raise himself to his knees. "Please, sheriff, don't kill me! I'm beggin' you!"

Buford Pusser laughed. He was not going to pull the trigger. That would have been too easy on Towhead White. Instead, Pusser forced the gangster to crawl around in the muddy swamp for several more hours. Then Buford drove Towhead back to the White Iris and dumped him.

Buford Pusser could never bury a grudge. He had a lasting thirst for revenge. His motto was "an eye for an eye and a tooth for a tooth."

Cathy Morris holds the handcuffs Buford Pusser placed on Towhead White when the sheriff took the gangster to the Hatchie River bottoms and "worked him over."

Early one morning in November 1964, Buford Pusser stopped to pick up a young hitchhiker along U.S. 45 near Selmer. As soon as the man got inside the car, he pulled a switchblade knife from his coat pocket and slammed it twice into Pusser's chest. Then the stranger leaped from the vehicle and ran away.

Buford drove himself to the McNairy County hospital. The doctors patched his wounds and then held him 24 hours for observation. Pusser had tasted violence a second time; he still carried the scars from his 1957 state-line beating.

Less than a month after the stabbing, Buford Pusser was called to a rural site where a house was burning. When firemen extinguished the flames, two charred bodies were found in the smoldering ruins. The house had burned so quickly that there had been no chance of rescuing the victims.

Moonshine stills flourished in McNairy County when Buford Pusser was elected sheriff. Pusser destroyed 87 illegal whiskey rigs in a single year.

As Pusser prepared to leave, he noticed an old Dodge parked a short distance away. The rear of the vehicle was almost touching the ground. Buford approached the side of the car, where a black man sat slouched under the steering wheel. "What you got in your trunk?" the sheriff asked.

"Nothin', man. Just the usual junk. You know. Tire, jack, tools, and stuff like that."

Pusser shook the automobile from side to side. He heard a sloshing sound coming from the rear compartment. "That stuff back there must be made of water instead of iron and metal from the way it sounds. Open the trunk!" Pusser demanded.

The sheriff decided to stroll around the car for a quick inspection while the suspected moonshiner got out and opened the trunk. But, when Pusser stepped in front of the automobile, the stranger started the engine and accelerated forward.

Clyde Garner operated the Stables Club in Henderson County, Tennessee, where Towhead White, Jack Hathcock, and other state-line mobsters were regular visitors.

Buford Pusser leaped into the air and landed spread-eagle on the hood. He held on to a radio aerial with his left hand while he reached through the side window and tried to snatch the keys from the ignition. "Stop this car! Stop it, you idiot!" Pusser yelled.

The driver ignored Pusser's screams but took a knife from his coat pocket and stabbed Buford five times. Meanwhile, the suspect's female companion slammed a pipe wrench against the lawman's head. Pusser slumped from the hood of the speeding car and sprawled backwards onto the gravel road.

Buford Pusser was transported to the McNairy County Memorial Hospital. His attackers' car was found abandoned two miles from the scene. A search of the vehicle revealed 31 gallons of moonshine in the trunk. The license plates on the automobile had been stolen. The identity of the couple was never ascertained. Pusser recovered with remarkable speed and was back on the job in less than two weeks.

Four months after Buford Pusser took office, the county commission granted his request for a full-time deputy. Buford hired Jim Moffett, a close friend, who lived near Stantonville. James Dickey had used only part-time deputies during his term in the sheriff's office.

Pusser and Moffett began hitting the state-line dives hard. They usually picked up a carload of drunks or bootleg whiskey on every trip. A visit to the Shamrock Motel always netted several gallons of moonshine. Pusser also waged a war on those who manufactured the illegal liquor. During his first year as sheriff, Buford raided 42 illicit whiskey stills and arrested more than 75 moonshiners.

Buford Pusser test fires his new .38-caliber Smith & Wesson snub-nosed pistol while his deputies watch. Standing, from left to right, are Deputy Sheriffs Willie Smith, T.W. Burks, and Peatie Plunk.

THE LEGACY OF BUFORD PUSSER

During Buford Pusser's second year in office, the county commissioners authorized him to hire another full-time deputy. Peatie Plunk joined Pusser's force.

The state-line raids increased as did the arrests for illegal whiskey making. McNairy County was slowly becoming a better place to live and raise a family.

As the end of Buford Pusser's first two-year term neared, he announced his candidacy for reelection. At that time, Tennessee sheriffs could seek only three two-year terms in office.

Pauline Pusser begged Buford to give up the idea of running for sheriff again. She wanted him to settle down to an ordinary life. He ignored her pleas.

Clifford Coleman, a Democrat who had been sheriff before James Dickey, was Pusser's major opponent in the campaign. The 1966 McNairy County sheriff's race commanded little attention, and Pusser defeated Coleman by a three-to-one margin.

Violence continued to stalk Buford Pusser. It was February 1, 1966, 10:15 in the morning, and Pusser was on his way to the Shamrock Motel to arrest Louise Hathcock. He had two warrants in his pocket, one for theft, the other for illegal possession of whiskey.

Pusser wheeled the sheriff's cruiser into the motel's parking area. Jim Moffett, chief deputy, shifted restlessly beside him. In the backseat, Peatie Plunk fumbled with his wide-brimmed hat.

The sheriff and his deputies were met by a young Illinois couple who had spent the night at the Shamrock. The man, young, wiry, and sandy-haired, explained to the officers that, when he went to pay his bill, Louise Hathcock robbed him of $125. "She told me to empty my wallet on the countertop. At first, I thought she was kidding. Then I realized she wasn't when a couple of big goons walked up beside her. She warned me that, if I called the law, my wife and I would both end up in the Tennessee River with a concrete block tied around our necks."

"Louise Hathcock wasn't kiddin'," the sheriff frowned. "A lot of other people she robbed did end up in the river."

Pusser asked the victims to sign the theft warrant. Then he and the deputies entered the motel office.

Louise Hathcock, sitting at a small desk behind the registration counter, was wearing a white duster and a pair of red house shoes. A glass nearly full of bourbon and Coke rested at the edge of her desk.

Louise looked up. Shock froze her face. The last person she was expecting to see was Buford Pusser.

"Got a warrant for your arrest, Louise. You've been charged with robbing a man and his wife of $125."

"I ain't clipped a soul out of anything. Where's the jerk at? He won't tell me that to my face!"

It was obvious to Pusser that Louise Hathcock had been drinking heavily. She must have been, he thought, hitting the bottle all night.

Pusser moved back from the counter. "Keep an eye on her, boys, while I look around."

Jim Moffett ordered Mrs. Hathcock from behind the reception counter.

A rearview look at the old McNairy County Courthouse in Selmer, Tennessee. The jail was on the top floor. Buford Pusser's office was located in the basement.

A Message from...

BUFORD PUSSER

Sheriff of McNairy County

DEAR FELLOW McNAIRY COUNTIANS:

As you already know. I was re-elected to the office of Sheriff of McNairy County in the August 4th election.

No greater compliment could be paid to a public official than to win by your overwhelming vote of confidence and I sincerely and humbly thank you for this endorsement and your continued support.

During the past two years we have endeavored to earn your confidence. I believe people have become proud of their Sheriff's Department and I want to emphatically commend them on their spirit and also all of my volunteers who have donated their tireless hours of service.

I hope that I have been able to lend sensible leadership to this important office. However, any credit due for progress and improvement—and I believe there has been a good deal of it—should go to the officers and city police who have given both dedicated and enthusiastic service to me and to you. Also, you my fellow McNairy Countians, are due a great deal of credit. My first two years have been an exciting and enlightening experience. I have learned a lot about being your Sheriff and the learning process continues each day. Problems remain to be solved but I willingly accept the challenge. It has been a good two years for me personally and I believe for the Sheriff's Department of McNairy County. With your continuing support, the next two should be even better.

Sincerely,

BUFORD PUSSER

SHERIFF OF McNAIRY COUNTY

On August 17, 1966, Buford Pusser ran this notice in the **McNairy County Consumer Guide.** *He had just been elected to his second term as sheriff.*

Louise Hathcock had a split personality. She would lend a helping hand to the needy one day, then murder a person in cold blood the next. Buford Pusser killed her in self-defense on February 1, 1966.
Copyrighted by W.R. Morris.

"Look, Moffett," she slurred. "I didn't rob that man and woman of a single penny. They're damned liars, both of 'em!"

"No use to talk to me about it," Moffett replied. "The sheriff is the boss."

"Yeah, I know. Big, bad Buford Pusser. He thinks this is Dodge City, and he's Matt Dillon," sneered Louise.

In a few minutes, Pusser returned, carrying a half-case of Yellowstone whiskey. "I'm also charging you with illegal possession of liquor in a dry county."

"Now listen, sheriff. I can explain this whole situation. Let's go to my private office, where we can talk without interruption."

"We can talk right here."

"No. I got some things to tell you that are confidential. I'm gonna level with you about the whole operation. I want to talk to you alone, though."

"Okay, but make it snappy."

"Let me get my drink. I need something to calm my nerves," said Louise as she walked to the desk to pick up the glass of whiskey with her left hand.

Pusser ordered Louise out of the office, then followed close behind to her private quarters. It was within those same walls that Louise's ex-husband, Jack Hathcock, had met his doom.

Pusser was surprised at the neatness of the room. Hangers of cleaned clothes in cellophane bags dangled from the inside doorknob. Louise attempted to shut the door, but the clothes swung between the lock and the catch. The door crept open. Slowly, Hathcock slid her right hand into her duster pocket and withdrew a .38-caliber pistol, the same revolver Towhead White had used to murder Jack Hathcock. Still holding the mixed drink in her left hand, she pointed the pistol at Buford Pusser. "You ain't takin' me nowhere!"

Louise Hathcock's gravestone.

Pusser jumped back, bumping the edge of the door as Louise fired. The impact from the collision with the door sprawled him across the bed. The bullet plowed plaster from the wall.

Louise Hathcock dropped her glass of whiskey to the green-carpeted floor and ran to the bed. Aiming her pistol directly at Pusser's head, she squeezed the trigger again. The click of the hammer striking the shell in the chamber sounded like a stick of dynamite exploding in Buford's ears. The bullet misfired.

Pusser scrambled to his knees on the bed, unholstered his .41-caliber magnum, and fired. The slug caught Louise in the left shoulder and spun her around. The second shot struck under her right arm, tearing a large hole through her heart and lungs. Mortally wounded, she raised her pistol again. Pusser's third shot plowed through Louise's left jaw. She clutched her chest with both hands, then slowly slumped to the floor.

Hearing the shots, Jim Moffett and Peatie Plunk rushed into the room. "You all right, Buford?" they asked in unison.

"Fine," Pusser mumbled. "But I wouldn't have been if her gun hadn't misfired."

Sheriff James Bishop arrested Towhead White on April 6, 1965, for making illegal whiskey in Tishomingo County, Mississippi. White received a three-year prison sentence.

Medical tests revealed that Louise Hathcock had .248 percent alcohol in her blood. Under Tennessee law, a blood alcohol level of .10 percent is enough to be legally intoxicated.

After checking the Tennessee Bureau of Investigation reports of the Louise Hathcock shooting, District Attorney Will T. Abernathy concluded that Buford Pusser had killed the state-line madam in self-defense. Nevertheless, Abernathy presented the case to the McNairy

Donald Lee Fulghum of Bethel Springs, Tennessee, displays the whiskey glass Louise Hathcock was holding when Buford Pusser shot her to death on February 1, 1966, at the Shamrock Motel.

Fulghum, a Selmer police officer who served nine years as chief, was a close friend of Pusser. "Buford was one of the toughest men I ever knew. He had nerves of solid steel," said Fulghum, "and he was as strong as an ox.

"I was riding with him one night when he received a call about a fight on Falcon Road in Selmer. When we arrived, there were four carloads of young men and teenagers arguing. Buford stepped out of his car and told everybody to hit the road. Three carloads left, but four guys in a Volkswagon ignored him.

"Buford walked over to the Volkswagon and picked it up from the ground, then dropped it. The occupants banged their heads together and were yelling in pain. Before the car even stopped bouncing, the driver was trying to get it started. They couldn't wait to get out of there," Fulghum laughed.

County grand jury for official action. The jurors ruled that Mrs. Hathcock's killing was justifiable homicide, and the case was closed.

The case was considered closed by law officials but not by Towhead White.

After Louise Hathcock's demise, Carl Douglas "Towhead" White marked Buford Pusser for death. He vowed to avenge the killing of his old girlfriend.

At the time, White was serving a three-year federal prison sentence at Leavenworth, Kansas, for participating in a three-state moonshine whiskey ring. No one, however, including police authorities, doubted White's ability to have outside connections do the job.

Late on January 2, 1967, Buford Pusser was shot by an assailant on U.S. 45 about three miles from the Tennessee-Mississippi border. He was struck by three .25-caliber bullets. None of the shots caused serious injury.

Towhead White, who had escaped on December 11, 1966, from a federal prison in Alabama, became a prime suspect. Two days after the attack on Pusser, White surrendered to prison authorities in Montgomery, Alabama. He refused to say where he had been or what he had done while he was a fugitive.

August 12, 1967. Saturday. The ringing telephone roused Buford Pusser from sleep. It was 4:30 a.m. "Hello," he answered drowsily.

"This Sheriff Pusser?" the caller inquired.

"Yessir."

"There's serious trouble brewin' on New Hope Road. Three or four drunks are threatenin' to shoot it out with each other. There's gonna be a killin' if ya don't hurry on down here!"

THE LEGACY OF BUFORD PUSSER

"I'm on my way."

Pusser quickly slid into his tan sheriff's uniform while his wife, Pauline, slipped into a pair of dark brown slacks, a white blouse, and black loafers. "I'm going with you, Buford. I'm already wide awake. And your mother is watching the kids," said Pauline.

The Pussers were looking forward to a family reunion with Pauline's relatives on Sunday. They were already packed and planning to leave for Haysi, Virginia, early the next day.

Buford Pusser touched the brakes, and Pauline grabbed a door handle as the Plymouth whipped onto New Hope Road.

Farmers were already in their barns – feeding and milking cows. In the east, redness was creeping into a cloudless sky, and the woods along the road were alive with morning sounds. "This is going to be a beautiful day," Pauline smiled. "Makes you want to live forever."

Up ahead, assassins waited in a sleek, black Cadillac. They were parked behind the New Hope Methodist Church and situated where they had a clear view of New Hope Road.

Pusser kept his eyes on the route before him. He was expecting to see trouble at any moment. In their concentration, neither he nor Pauline saw or heard the black Cadillac approaching from behind.

"We ought to be gettin' close to the spot where the trouble's supposed to be," said the sheriff, turning the steering wheel to dodge a large hole in the road.

Suddenly, the Pussers heard the roar of an engine, and the long, black car was beside them. Orange flames belched from

Pauline Pusser.

Kirskey Nix, Jr., and his gunmen were hiding behind the New Hope Methodist Church as they waited for Sheriff Pusser's car to pass. They ambushed the Pussers, killing Pauline and gravely wounding Buford.

55

a .30-caliber carbine. The window on the driver's side of Pusser's car shattered, spraying his face with slivers of glass. The shots missed him and slammed into Pauline's head. She moaned, grabbing her husband's arm as she slumped down in the seat.

Pusser floorboarded the Plymouth. His only thought was escape. He had to get help for his dying wife. Pusser knew that he did not have a chance against the assassins in the semidarkness.

He drove two miles down the road and skidded to a stop, thinking that he had escaped the killers. Gently, Buford placed Pauline's head on his lap. When he saw the gaping hole in her head, he was sick with fright and rage. "Oh, God, please don't let her die! Please, God, don't let her die!" Pusser prayed aloud.

Then the black Cadillac appeared again. This time, a volley of shots riddled the car at point-blank range. Pusser caught two slugs in the lower jaw, and his whole chin dropped to his chest, held only by a flap of skin. He sank to the floorboard as another bullet ripped through the metal door and shattered Pauline's skull. Blood soaked the seats, the floorboard, and the occupants.

The ambushers fled, thinking that both Buford Pusser and his wife were dead. Buford looked at Pauline and knew at once that the thugs had killed her.

Although Pusser was critically wounded, he placed his hand on his wife's warm cheek and promised to avenge her murder. "I do love you, Pauline. Only God knows how much I love you. They'll pay for what they done to you. This I promise!" he mumbled.

Buford Pusser was taken to the medical facility in Selmer, then transferred to Baptist Hospital in Memphis. Shelby County sheriff's deputies, fearing the assassins might return to finish their job, stood guard outside the door of Pusser's hospital room around the clock.

State, county, and federal law-enforcement officers swarmed the ambush sites on New Hope Road. Authorities found 14 empty .30-caliber cartridge cases. The bullets used in the attack all contained soft-nosed lead slugs. Chief Deputy Sheriff Jim Moffett and TBI Agent Warren Jones found 11 bullet holes in Pusser's Plymouth.

The investigators concluded that the ambush was motivated by Buford Pusser's campaign to clean up illegal activities on the state line. The shooting of Louise Hathcock and the possible involvement of Towhead White were mentioned.

A few hours after the ambush, rumors circulated in McNairy County that Buford Pusser had murdered his wife and then shot himself to cover up the crime.

Fred Plunk, owner of a tavern and barbecue place near the Hardin-McNairy county line, scoffed at the talk. "I've known Buford almost all his life. He didn't shoot Pauline any more than I did. The lower part of his face was blown completely off. Nobody's going to do that to himself. He's lucky to be alive."

The authorities investigating the New Hope Road tragedy shared the same opinion.

Eighteen days after the slaying, Buford Pusser went home. While he was in the hospital, Pauline had been laid to rest in the Adamsville Cemetery.

Although plastic surgeon Rufus Cravens had worked long and hard on his patient – cutting, stitching, and wiring bones and teeth – Pusser's face remained scarred and broken. The Memphis doctor said Pusser's jaw had been struck by at least two high-powered bullets and possibly three.

Buford Pusser, bitter and vindictive, launched his own investigation into his wife's murder. He wanted to personally deal with the killers – man-to-man, face-to-face.

He learned that Towhead White, from his prison cell, had sealed a "kiss of death" contract on the sheriff with Dixie Mafia kingpin Kirksey McCord Nix, Jr. Nix, the son of an Oklahoma appellate court judge, was one of the most dangerous criminals in the southwestern part of the United States. Nix and White played in the same league.

The Oklahoma-born gangster had handpicked three other professionals for the Buford Pusser murder team: Carmine Raymond Gagliardi (a Boston thug with mob ties in the East) and Dixie Mafia hit men George Allen McGann and Gary Elbert McDaniel.

Towhead White bristled with anger each time he thought about Pusser's "stroke of pure luck." The big lawman was supposed to be dead. White marveled at the fact that Buford Pusser was still breathing. He kept asking himself how the sheriff had survived the barrage of high-powered rifle slugs that ripped away half of his face and left his wife a corpse beside him.

Helen Pusser made an effort to tell Buford about his wife's

This bullet hole through the windshield of Buford Pusser's Plymouth is a grim reminder of the tragedy that occurred on August 12, 1967.

THE LEGACY OF BUFORD PUSSER

Jim Moffett, McNairy County's chief deputy sheriff, inspects the 1967 Plymouth Fury in which Pauline Pusser was murdered and Buford was left on the threshold of death.

Curiosity seekers mingle with law-enforcement officers at a site on New Hope Road in rural McNairy County where assassins killed Pauline Pusser and seriously hurt Sheriff Pusser.

THE LEGACY OF BUFORD PUSSER

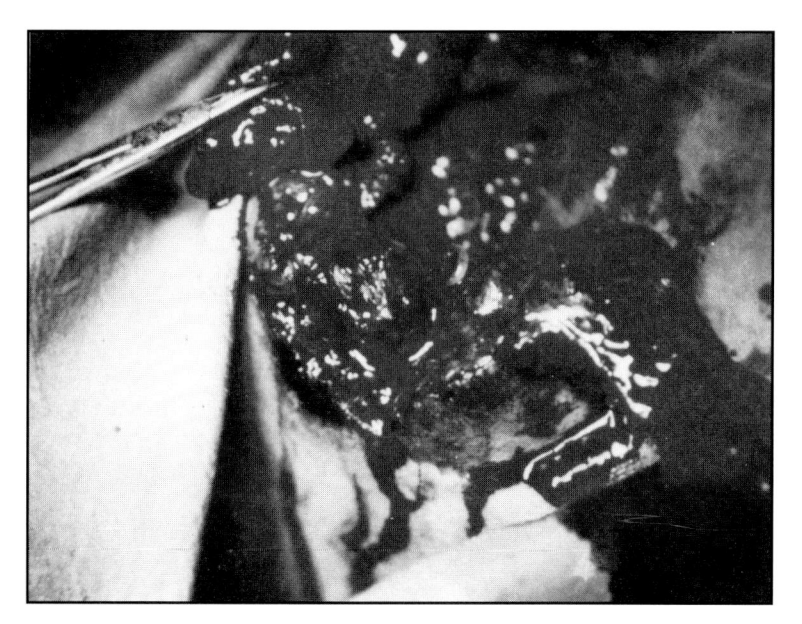

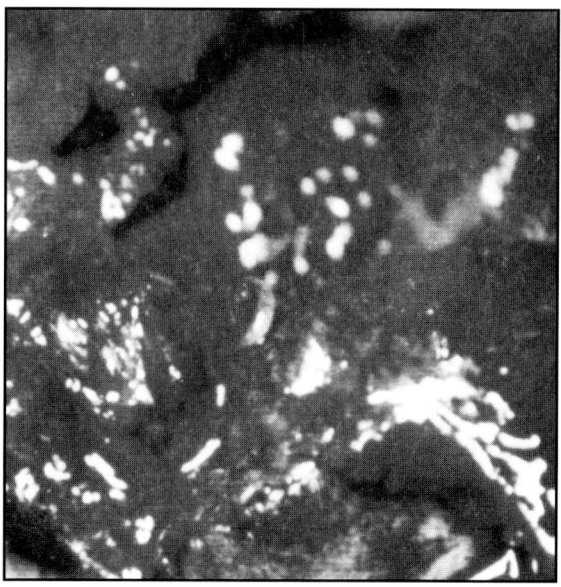

These photographs of Buford Pusser's face prove absurd the theory that he killed his wife, then shot himself to cover up the crime. "Sheriff Pusser, in his critical condition, could not have disposed of the weapons and the other evidence after the ambush," said a state agent who investigated Pauline Pusser's murder. The doctor who performed emergency surgery on Pusser said the sheriff's jaw was struck by two high-powered rifle bullets and possibly three.
Photos copyrighted by W.R. Morris.

funeral. She informed him that James Hall, an Adamsville postal worker, had taped the services. But Buford refused to listen to the recording or hear any details about the funeral. He had no desire to experience the service. He was still in a vacuum of bitterness and disbelief.

After the New Hope ambush, Buford Pusser changed his style of dress. Instead of his usual tan sheriff's uniform, he wore tailored suits, colorful ties, and immaculate white shirts. He thought he would be less conspicuous in street clothes. He also traded cars often, seldom driving the same one for more than a month.

Moreover, Buford Pusser armed himself to meet any situation. He replaced his automatic 12-gauge shotgun with an M-16 carbine. He retired his old .41-caliber magnum to a trophy case and holstered a new .357 magnum.

Pusser was frightened. He lived daily in the shadow of fear – fear that the assassins would return to complete the task they had only half done on the morning of August 12, 1967. But he was determined to find them first.

The incredible true story of Sheriff Buford Pusser, the Tennessee giant who blasted organized crime out of his territory! Hero of the sensational film **Walking Tall**

A BCP PRODUCTION

ELIZABETH HARTMAN AND JOE DON BAKER,

The Twelfth of August
by W. R. Morris
ILLUSTRATED WITH PHOTOGRAPHS

After his wife's death, Buford Pusser wore a special ring on the little finger of his left hand. The cluster of stones that adorned it were taken from Pauline's engagement ring and wedding band, her dinner ring, and a smaller ring she had worn.

Buford Pusser in 1967 before plastic surgeons completely rebuilt his bullet-shattered face. Pusser underwent 16 facial operations to restore his lower jaw following the New Hope Road ambush that left his wife a corpse.

Kirskey McCord Nix, Jr., was named by Buford Pusser as the chief executioner in his wife's murder. Nix is currently serving life without parole in a Louisiana prison for killing a New Orleans grocer. He was also convicted for conspiracy in the gangland-styled slayings of Circuit Judge Vincent Sherry and his wife in Biloxi, Mississippi.

Pusser's search for Pauline's killers was temporarily interrupted on February 26, 1968, when he learned from Alcorn County, Mississippi, authorities that Paul David English, an escapee from the McNairy County jail, had been sighted in Corinth. The 22-year-old English, awaiting trial for first-degree murder, had been on the run for several days. It was the second time he had fled the jail.

In September 1967, English slid down a rope to freedom from the third floor of the county lockup. His girlfriend had smuggled him the rope and a hacksaw blade. A couple of days later, he surrendered.

On February 26, 1968, after he had escaped from the McNairy County Jail, Paul David English was shot and paralyzed by Buford Pusser. Today, English walks with a limp but works full-time at a convenience store.

Buford Pusser considered Paul David English, a relative of the Hathcocks (Jack Hathcock was his mother's first cousin), a genuine troublemaker.

When Pusser arrived in Corinth, he met Police Chief Art Murphy. The chief climbed into the sheriff's new Oldsmobile Toronado and informed the McNairy County lawman that English was driving a dark-colored 1956 Bel Aire Chevrolet.

Minutes later, Pusser and Murphy spotted English cruising west on Proper Street. They could not believe their good luck. As the officers approached English from the rear, he recognized Pusser's Olds and floorboarded the Chevy. The fugitive sped through Corinth and headed north up Wenasoga Road. Pusser, with a portable blue light flashing on his dashboard, remained close behind. English fed the old Chevrolet all the gas it could swallow. He fought the steering wheel to maintain control of the car. It was obvious that the outlaw had no intention of stopping.

Buford Pusser grabbed his M-16 carbine from a rack beside him. "Keep the car in the road, Art. I'm going to stop English one way or the other," Pusser vowed.

Murphy scooted across the seat toward the sheriff and grasped the steering wheel. "Damn, Buford, be careful," cautioned Murphy. "We don't want to wreck!"

Pusser leaned out the window, aimed the rifle, and fired three times. One bullet tore through the trunk, ripped through the backseat, and slammed into Paul David English's spine. The fugitive managed to skid the Chevy to a stop. Pusser, still holding the M-16 carbine in his left hand, ran up, jerked open the car door, and ordered English to exit the vehicle.

The murder suspect wailed, "I can't get out! I can't move my legs! The pain is killing me!"

Pusser knew at once that English was paralyzed. Why, he asked himself, had the outlaw forced him to pull the trigger? This would never have happened if the fugitive had just surrendered peacefully.

Paul David English was taken to the Corinth hospital and then transferred to a medical facility in Memphis, Tennessee. Doctors first predicted that English would never walk again. He was laid up in the hospital for six months and 17 days. During English's confinement, Buford Pusser visited him several times. After a series of operations and much physical therapy, English finally did manage to walk.

Once released from the hospital, he stood trial for murder. He was convicted and served 35 months of a 10-year sentence. No charges were ever filed against him for escaping from jail. Today, Paul David English still walks with a limp, but he does work full-time at a convenience store in McNairy County.

Buford Pusser traced Carmine Raymond Gagliardi, one of his wife's assassins, to Boston. Before the McNairy County sheriff could nab him, the gangster was found shot to death near Boston Harbor.

The big lawman still had other members of the murder squad with whom to deal. And he would never enjoy a moment's peace until all of them had paid for their horrible deeds.

Buford Pusser seldom displayed his emotions; instead he kept his thoughts and feelings locked inside. After Pauline's death, he often became depressed and moody.

The sheriff's morale was boosted somewhat when Eddie Bond, a Memphis singer, released a record entitled "The Ballad of Buford Pusser." Several thousand copies were sold. Carl Pusser even peddled the ballad at the jail. The McNairy County lockup became a record shop with one label in stock.

Buford Pusser won the 1968 sheriff's race by a two-to-one margin over William Littlejohn without so much as a campaign speech. He hoped this term would be less chaotic.

Violence, however, seemed to be Pusser's constant companion. On Christmas Day, 1968, he was forced to kill Charles Russell Hamilton. Don Pipkin, Hamilton's cousin, had called Pusser to report that his relative was drunk and threatening to shoot Pipkin and his wife.

The sheriff considered the 50-year-old Hamilton to be a heartless killer who should have been strapped into the electric chair years ago. Hamilton had slit his mother-in-law's throat, shot a deputy sheriff in Alabama, and murdered his own wife. In addition to that, he had stabbed another inmate in prison and knifed a man to death in a tavern brawl. Now, he was working for the McNairy County Highway Department.

Pusser parked his car in front of Hamilton's apartment and got out. He adjusted his .357 magnum in a holster on his alligator belt, then stepped up onto the porch and knocked on the door.

"Come in," said a polite voice.

As the sheriff entered the room, Hamilton began shooting his .32-caliber automatic. One slug streaked across the lawman's abdomen. A second whizzed past his head. And a third clipped the handle of his holstered magnum. Two more slugs slammed into the wall.

Pusser swiftly unholstered his pistol and fired. The bullet smashed Hamilton between the eyes and tore through the back of his head. Pusser had killed his second person.

The case, like that concerning the shooting of Louise Hathcock,

Helen Pusser stands in front of the 1968 Oldsmobile Toronado that Buford Pusser was driving when he shot and paralyzed Paul David English after a jail escape.

THE LEGACY OF BUFORD PUSSER

Deputies Willie Smith and Peatie Plunk and Sheriff Buford Pusser. The 1968 Pontiac was Pusser's official patrol car.

The old door from Buford Pusser's office, which was located in the basement of the McNairy County Courthouse.

Paul Moore operated Moore's Place in Michie, Tennessee, during Buford Pusser's reign as sheriff. "Buford was always polite unless someone gave him a reason to be otherwise," said Moore.

was turned over to the McNairy County grand jury by District Attorney Will T. Abernathy. As in the Hathcock slaying, the jurors ruled that Pusser had shot in self-defense.

Buford Pusser received some good news on April 2, 1969. One of his most bitter enemies was dead. Carl Douglas "Towhead" White had been murdered just after midnight at the El-Ray Motel in Corinth.

Shirley Smith was a passenger in White's Chrysler when he parked it in front of the motel and an assassin opened fire. Shirley, the wife of state-line mobster Berry "Junior" Smith, somehow escaped unharmed.

The hit man, lying on the roof, had skillfully triggered a .30-.30 rifle slug through the windshield and into White's forehead. Blood gushed from an ugly bullet hole just above Towhead's eyebrows. His brown eyes were wide open. In the motel parking area, several more shots echoed in the still night air.

Roland Johnson, mayor of Hanceville, Alabama, (left) and Buford Pusser in 1970. The mayor, a country music singer and songwriter, gives Buford a copy of one of his records.

Eddie Bond, a country music singer from Memphis, was the first to record a Buford Pusser song. Bond's rendition, "The Ballad of Buford Pusser," was well accepted in the South after its release in 1968. The song was written by Memphis disc jockey Jim Climer.

Lawton Williams, a Fort Worth, Texas, songwriter, wrote and recorded "The McNairy County Sheriff." Williams has penned several hit songs, including "Farewell Party" for Gene Watson.

Almost before the gunsmoke had settled, Alcorn County Sheriff Grady Bingham and his brother, Chief Deputy Hobert Bingham, arrived on the scene. "What's goin' on here, Junior?" the sheriff asked.

"I think I've killed Towhead White. He was drunk and shot at me," claimed Smith. "He shot first."

"Well, you're under arrest for murder. Get in the car," Grady Bingham snapped.

At the jail, Junior Smith told the sheriff that the shooting had erupted when White and Shirley arrived at the motel and White began cursing him and firing at him with a pistol. Smith said he ducked, then turned and ran into the office of the motel, where he grabbed the .30-.30 rifle. Next, he leveled the rifle at White's two-door green Chrysler. According to Smith, when his wife saw the rifle aimed at the car, she struggled to get the passenger door open. When she failed, she took cover on the floorboard just as a bullet shattered the windshield. Shirley Smith finally pushed open the door and leaped from the automobile. Smith claimed he then jerked a .357 magnum from his belt and drilled three holes through the passenger door of the vehicle.

White's car had been riddled by nine bullets; six were rifle slugs.

After an investigation, Sheriff Grady Bingham was convinced that Junior Smith had not killed Towhead White. Smith's story about the slaying had more holes in it than the late gangster's bullet-riddled Chrysler did. The fatal shot through the windshield was fired down from a high angle, not from ground level as Smith had claimed. The .38-caliber pistol was removed from White's left hand although he was right-handed. An examination revealed only two spent cartridges in the cylinder. Grady Bingham said the revolver was definitely placed in White's hand after he had died.

Furthermore, the pistol was registered to Shirley Smith. Investigators failed to locate any other guns on White or in his car.

Rumors quickly spread that Buford Pusser had instigated the state-line kingpin's murder.

"I didn't shoot Towhead White. I would have shot him if he had ever given me the opportunity," said Pusser. "White was like a poisonous snake. He needed killing."

Almost everyone agreed, however, that Pusser had masterminded White's death. The sheriff had vowed for two years to even the score with White for the ambush that left the lawman's wife a corpse and him on the threshold of death.

Berry "Junior" Smith kept insisting that he did kill Carl Douglas "Towhead" White in self-defense. The Alcorn County grand jury agreed.

Actually, none of the law-enforcement officers had really tried to unearth the true facts surrounding White's murder. They were just happy that another big-time criminal was out of circulation.

Buford Pusser took a short leave of absence from his sheriff's duties on February 22, 1970, to attend the annual Tennessee Jaycees convention in Gatlinburg. Pusser had agreed to personally appear at the event to receive one of the three "Outstanding Young Men of the Year" awards from the Jaycees.

"The Tennessee Jaycees tonight are proud to announce the selection of McNairy County Sheriff Buford Pusser as one of the state's outstanding young men of 1969. Buford, a renowned and respected sheriff, is being honored for his relentless pursuit of law and order," the emcee smiled.

Shortly after the Jaycees paid homage to Pusser, rumors circulated that he planned to seek the governor's chair. Several state newspapers carried stories saying that the colorful sheriff was planning to become a candidate for the office.

Finally, on May 29, 1970, during a press conference in Memphis, Pusser said he was not a candidate for governor and announced his endorsement of State House Speaker Bill Jenkins, a Republican, who was seeking his party's nomination.

But Winfield Dunn, a Memphis dentist, won the gubernatorial slot on the GOP ticket that year. And Clifford Coleman defeated six other candidates to win the McNairy County sheriff's race. Buford Pusser was prohibited by state law from seeking another term in the sheriff's office that year. In Adamsville, however, he was elected constable of the Third Civil District by more than 84 write-in votes. Raymond Gray, who was seeking reelection to the post, received 60 votes.

Parolee, Tagged As 'Top Hood', Is Slain At Motel

By EDWARD ARNOLD
From The Commercial Appeal
Northeast Miss., Bureau

CORINTH, Miss., April 3. — A 35-year-old federal prison parolee, Carl Douglas 'Towhead' White, described by the FBI as "one of the top hoods in the Southeast" was shot to death near a Corinth motel early Thursday morning.

Beside White's bullet-riddled body in a car outside El-Ray Motel, was a pistol with two spent cartridges.

Berry 'Junior' Smith, 35, co-owner of the motel was taken into custody after the shooting. Smith told officers White fired the first shots.

Alcorn County Atty. Horace Brewer said, "It really doesn't look like there are going to be any charges filed. It just looks like a case of self-defense so far and no charges will be filed unless an investigation discloses evidence to the contrary."

White had a long criminal record. He was arrested in Memphis in 1963 on a warrant from Meridian, Miss., charging embezzlement and was accused of selling 33 imitation diamonds for $10,000. He was previously arrested in Memphis on parole violation charges and armed robbery on warrants from Corinth, Miss.

Carl D. White

White was among five persons indicted in connection with the $11,000 armed robbery in 1965 of the former Red Carpet Gambling Casino in Biloxi.

White also was convicted in Circuit Court at Corinth in 1967 for contempt of court on charges he tampered with a jury. White was paroled three months ago from the federal penitentiary at Leavenworth, Kan., where he was serving a three-year sentence for violation of liquor laws.

Earlier this week, Clarksdale Police Chief Ben Collins was suspended by city officials after a commissioner accused the police chief of having links with White in the juke box business.

White had lived in Clarksdale several weeks, moving there from Corinth.

Sheriff Buford Pusser of McNairy County, Tenn., said, "We have done a lot of investigating on White. He was one of the leaders of crime operations near the stateline between McNairy and Alcorn Counties." White was among Sheriff Pusser's suspects for the shooting death of the sheriff's wife on a lonely rural Tennessee road three years ago. Sheriff Pusser was himself wounded in the ambush-type shooting.

Smith's motel has been raided several times recently. He and his wife, Mrs. Shirley Smith, had been arrested on charges of illegal storage of intoxicating liquor and possession of liquor for resale.

Smith and his wife also operated the Nightfall Motel, separated from the El-Ray by a restaurant.

White owned White's Amusement Center on Highway 72 at the Mississippi-Tennessee line near here.

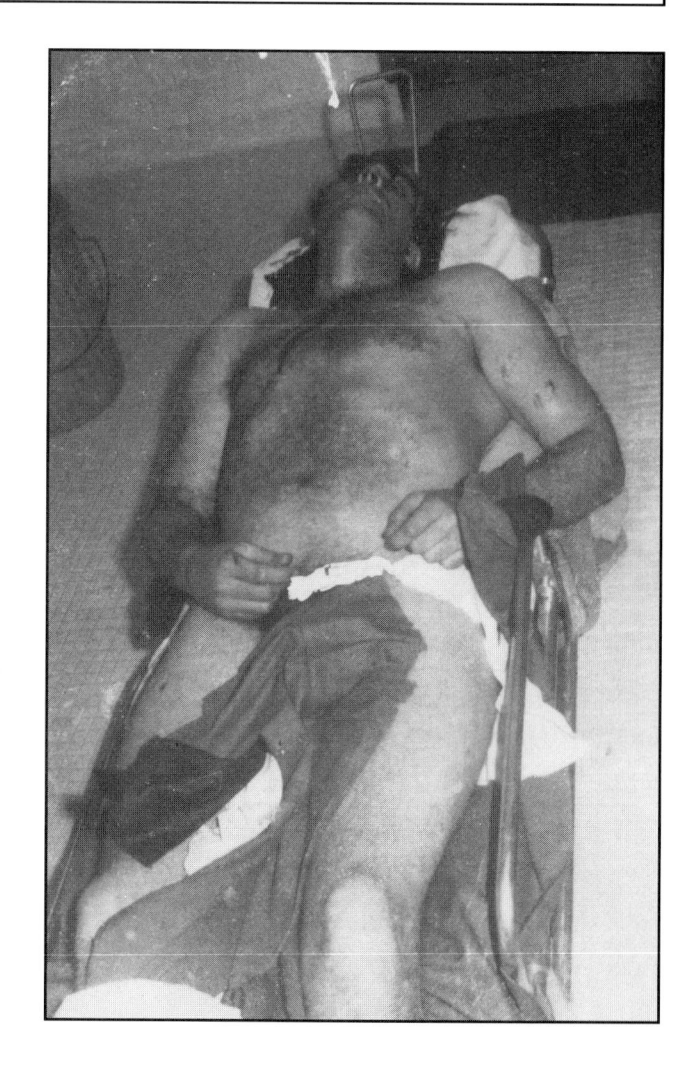

Towhead White was murdered on April 2, 1969, at the El Ray Motel in Corinth, Mississippi. His bullet-riddled corpse lay on a gurney at the Coleman Funeral Home there.

APRIL 4, 1969

'Junior' Smith Charged With White's Murder

Alcorn County Sheriff Grady Bingham reported this morning that Berry (Junior) Smith Jr., 35, has been charged with the murder of Carl Douglas (Towhead) White.

Bingham said it had been reported earlier that Smith was being held and that charges had not been placed.

However, this morning the sheriff said that Smith was charged with murder when he was brought in after the fatal shooting late Wednesday night.

The sheriff said a preliminary hearing has been set for 10 a.m. Saturday before Justice of the Peace M. B. Brawner. Smith's bond has been set at $5,000.

Alcorn County Attorney Horace Brewer said, "It just looks like a case of self defense so far."

Sheriff Bingham said Smith admitted killing White, but claimed he fired in self defense after White shot at him twice with a pistol.

The altercation occurred late Wednesday night in front of the El-Ray Motel on Highway 45 South, less than a mile from the Corinth city limits.

Funeral services for White were set for 4:30 p.m. today at National Funeral Home in Clarksdale, Miss., with the Rev. Leroy Tubbs of Clarksdale officiating. Burial will be in Memorial Gardens Cemetery, Clarksdale.

A native of Sumner, Miss., White's age was listed as 32 and his home address was given as 1902 Londonderry St., Corinth.

He is survived by his mother, Mrs. Elizabeth White, of Corinth; and three sisters, Mrs. John P. Wells, Jackson, Miss., Mrs. Rachel Beard, Clarksdale, Miss., and Pat White, Corinth.

White was killed around midnight Wednesday while he sat in a 1969 green Chrysler with Smith's estranged wife, Mrs. Shirley Smith, at the El-Ray Motel.

Sheriff Bingham said six rounds from a 30-30 caliber rifle were fired into the car with shots hitting White in the head, chest and arm. The sheriff noted that the fatal shot was apparently the first one fired.

Bingham said Smith told officers he had returned from a trip into Tennessee and saw White and his (Smith's) wife sitting in the car. He said White shot at him from the car and he ducked into the motel office and got a rifle.

White allegedly fired a second time, then Smith said he returned the fire with the rifle. Officers said the car was riddled with about six slugs from a 30-30 rifle.

A .38 caliber pistol that Bingham said had been fired twice was found in White's hand.

Authorities said White had a lengthy police record and was described by a veteran law enforcement officer as "one of the top hoods in the southeastern part of the United States."

According to information compiled by the Federal Bureau of Investigation, White was in the U.S. Air Force in 1952 and the U.S. Army in 1953. He was inducted both times in Jackson, Miss.

The FBI report lists the following activities of White:

"In August of 1954 he was picked up by the FBI in Butte, Montana, as a deserter fugitive.

"In March of 1956 he was arrested in Corinth, Miss., and charged with public drunkeness. In June, he was held as a material witness in an unspecified crime in Gretna, La. In July, he was arrested by the Columbus, Miss. Police Department and charged with palpable jury. He was arrested in December by the Clarksdale Police Department for investigation.

"In June of 1957 the sheriff's office in El Paso, Tex., arrested him and he was charged and convicted of hitchiking. Two days later a U.S. Marshal in El Paso took him over on a warrant charging unlawful flight to avoid prosecution.

"In September of 1957 he was installed in Parchman on conviction of two counts of burglary in Quitman County. He was sentenced to two years on one count and three on the other to run consecutively.

"In November of 1961 he was arrested by the Memphis Police Department for parole violation. In December of 1961 he was charged by the Memphis Police Department with parole violation and was referred back to Parchman.

"In January of 1962 he was reinstalled at Parchman to run out the Quitman County sentences on two counts of burglary.

"In mid-1962 the Kenosha, Wisc., Police Department arrested him and charged him with 'C.C.W.' and no drivers license.

"In December of 1962 he was arrested by the Memphis Police Department as a fugitive and referred to the Shelby County Jail.

Former Alcorn County Sheriff Grady Bingham investigated the murder of Towhead White. Bingham insists that Junior Smith, who confessed to slaying White, was not the triggerman.

On August 31, 1970, Buford Pusser gathered a few personal belongings, then switched off the light and strolled out the office door. The next day, McNairy County would have a new sheriff.

For a few days after leaving office, Pusser enjoyed the serenity of his home. One evening, as he lay on the couch in his den, he gazed at the diamond ring on the small finger of his left hand. The cluster of stones that adorned it had been taken from Pauline's engagement ring and wedding band, her dinner ring, and a smaller ring she had worn. Shortly after his wife was murdered, Pusser had a jeweler fashion the ring for him. It was a constant reminder that he still had a score to settle.

Kirksey McCord Nix, Jr., chief executioner in the murder of Pauline Pusser, was currently in prison for another slaying, and Pusser was patiently waiting for him to make parole. The other four conspirators involved in the New Hope Road ambush had suffered untimely deaths from unnatural causes. Towhead White, who plotted and bankrolled the ambush, had met a violent death in Corinth. Carmine Raymond Gagliardi, an East Coast thug, had been shot to death and tossed into Boston Harbor. And George Allen McGann and Gary Elbert McDaniel, the two Dixie Mafia hit men recruited to the Pusser assassination team by Nix, had both been found riddled with gangster bullets in Texas.

Whenever he considered the fates of the slain assassins, Buford Pusser found the demise of Towhead White the most gratifying. Pusser had hated the gangster with a vehement passion.

Pusser often smiled when he remembered the night he drilled White's house trailer with machine-gun bullets while the outlaw was lying in bed. White had pressed his body flat against the mattress, a maneuver he credited with saving his life.

Before leaving, Pusser placed a huge death wreath on Towhead's front door. Shaken, the thug left home. Three nights in a row, White hid in a ditch across from his dwelling. He was armed with a high-powered rifle – waiting for Buford Pusser to return. Pusser never showed.

T.W. Burks served as deputy sheriff under Buford Pusser and continued in law enforcement after Pusser left office. In 1977, Burks was elected "Officer of the Year" by the Fraternal Order of Police.

THE LEGACY OF BUFORD PUSSER

Abby Funderburk of Lexington, Tennessee, displays the license plate Buford Pusser had on his sheriff's car in 1969.

Buford Pusser in Birmingham, Alabama, in 1972.

Buford Pusser enjoyed his unemployment status for a couple of weeks; then he hit the campaign trail for Winfield Dunn. Pusser's first choice, Bill Jenkins, had been defeated by Dunn in the Republican primary. But Pusser was convinced that Dunn would make a fine chief executive for his state. At the Scenic Club in Knoxville, Pusser was a guest speaker, and he helped raise $25,000 for the Dunn coffers. The ex-sheriff spent weeks traveling Tennessee to promote the Republican nominee for governor. Winfield Dunn coasted to an easy victory over Democrat John Jay Hooker. Pusser was justifiably proud of the part he had played.

Buford Pusser was soon involved in more exciting news. The officials of Bing Crosby Productions were on their way to McNairy County to sign a movie contract with him.

Within weeks, Hollywood crews were busy filming scenes depicting the life of Buford Pusser. The motion picture, entitled "Walking Tall," was to star Joe Don Baker as Buford and Elizabeth Hartman as Pauline.

In the meantime, Pusser had jumped into the 1972 McNairy County sheriff's race with both feet. Clifford Coleman was determined

77

Buford Pusser and his mother, Helen, in the backyard at his Adamsville home.

THE LEGACY OF BUFORD PUSSER

Buford Pusser after 16 operations restored his bullet-shattered face.

mined to keep the job. Buford Pusser was just as firmly resolved to unseat him.

Both Coleman and Pusser fought tireless campaigns. When the political dust finally settled, Coleman defeated Pusser 3,934 votes to 3,251.

Buford Pusser, a man said to be cold and unemotional, wept. He blamed the movie issue for the loss. Many folks in McNairy County were down on Pusser because "Walking Tall" was being filmed in Chester and Madison Counties.

Pusser believed that Clifford Coleman had thrown cold water on the idea of filming in McNairy County by refusing to allow Bing Crosby Productions the use of the jail facilities. That, however, was not true. While Coleman did not go out of his way to encourage the movie making, neither did he make an all-out effort to squelch it. Because Coleman and Pusser were engaged in a battle for the sheriff's office, Bing Crosby officials assumed that Coleman would not cooperate with them. They never bothered to ask for his help.

After all, Selmer Mayor Billy Joe Glover, whom Buford Pusser despised, had already slammed the door shut in Hollywood's face. Instead of worrying about what was in the best interest of the city, Glover was concerned with hurting Pusser. The mayor flushed the movie's economic value to Selmer down the drain while he wallowed in personal satisfaction.

When "Walking Tall" hit the theaters in cities across the United States early in 1973, it was a box-office flop. The film played three weeks to sparse crowds in Los Angeles, then headed for burial. The same happened elsewhere.

Bing Crosby officials scurried feverishly to come up with new promotional schemes. The original ad material had stressed raw violence. Therefore, many parents refused to take their youngsters to see the film.

A new advertising campaign was launched. It played down the violence and played up the fact that the movie was a story about a young man who refused to surrender to the system and the woman who always stood by him. The promos also leaned heavily on the claim that the motion picture was a true story.

Shortly after the new promotions were unveiled, record-breaking crowds flocked to the Park Theater in Memphis, Tennessee, during the film's opening days there. That theater was credited with playing a major role in turning "Walking Tall" around after disappointing engagements elsewhere.

McNairy Countians who knew Buford Pusser discredited the legitimacy of the movie. They considered Joe Don Baker's film portrayal of Pusser using a big stick to maintain law and order a joke. Everyone familiar with Buford's law-enforcement tactics knew he never carried a stick. Hollywood had drowned the real Pusser story in fiction ink. Nonetheless, the "Walking Tall" movie continued to break box-office records across the United States.

W.R. Morris, Buford Pusser, and a fan at an autograph session for **The Twelfth of August** *in Corinth, Mississippi, in 1971.*

Governor Winfield Dunn issued a proclamation setting aside October 21, 1973, as a day for all Tennesseans to honor the sheriff who had gained national recognition and bestowed pride upon the state. The United States Senate also passed a resolution honoring Buford Pusser.

A three-day celebration got underway in Adamsville on October 19. The major attractions were Grand Ole Opry stars George Jones, Tammy Wynette, Johnny Paycheck, Patsy Sledge, Harold Morrison, and Lynn Anderson. A wrestling match featuring Jackie Fargo and the Masked Marvel was also on the agenda. Promoters had stimulated interest by arranging for Buford Pusser to referee the bout.

The legendary sheriff arrived early on opening day and posed for photographs with several politicians, including U.S. Congressman Robin Beard, Tennessee Speaker of the House Ned McWherter, and Lieutenant Governor John Wilder.

Pusser introduced all the guests to his date, Anne Randle Galloway. The slender, blue-eyed brunette was a 19-year-old pianist from Knoxville and the reigning Miss Tennessee. Rumors had circulated for weeks that she and Pusser were secretly engaged and would soon be married. Pusser neither denied nor confirmed the reports.

One of Buford Pusser's greatest fascinations was politics. Although he would not admit it, he relished every minute he spent on the campaign trail.

Early in 1974, the ex-lawman stumped throughout the Tennessee countryside asking voters to put Ray Blanton in the governor's office. Pusser did not really want to lend his name and support to Blanton. A born Republican, he favored GOP candidate Lamar Alexander. But pressure from close friends had cast Pusser into his present role. After all, he and Blanton had gone to school together and been friends and neighbors for years. Leonard Blanton, Ray's father, had given Buford his first law-enforcement job when the elder Blanton was mayor of Adamsville.

In shopping centers and in front of courthouses, Buford Pusser preached the same message in his soft-spoken Southern voice. "I want y'all to walk tall with Ray Blanton. He's the man we need for our next governor. Let's all get behind Ray Blanton and make him governor of Tennessee."

The throngs would cheer loud and long.

Pusser campaigned for Blanton in 60 of Tennessee's 95 counties, drawing record crowds. The whirlwind tour paid off. Ray Blanton easily

THE LEGACY OF BUFORD PUSSER

Buford Pusser and evangelist Billy Graham were among the guests at Johnny Cash's Hendersonville, Tennessee, home on November 24, 1973. From left to right, Pusser, Graham, Cash, John Rollin, Nat Winston, and James Neal.

defeated 10 other challengers to win the Democratic nomination. Lamar Alexander received the Republican nod. Blanton would later be elected governor.

Shortly after the primary elections, Bing Crosby Productions informed Buford Pusser they planned to film a second picture based upon his life. But they were having problems getting Joe Don Baker to sign a contract to play Pusser in the "Walking Tall" sequel. Baker claimed he had been ripped off by Bing Crosby Productions. The actor refused to elaborate. Finally, however, he spurned all offers.

With Baker's name scratched from the list, movie officials decided to salvage the next installment of the "Walking Tall" story by casting Buford Pusser to play himself. After all, millions had

Buford Pusser in July 1974.

WASHINGTON, TUESDAY, OCTOBER 30, 1973

Senate

MR. BROCK. Mr. President, it is not too often that one gets the opportunity to honor a "living legend," but we have the opportunity before us. The man is Buford Pusser. He is the former sheriff of McNairy County in Tennessee. During his terms in office, this man gained the reputation as one of the most effective crime fighters in the United States. He attacked organized crime in his county with a passion seldom seen in modern time.

The results were startling. On numerous occasions, Buford Pusser was the target of attempts on his life. Twice, he was left for dead, in critical condition. During one of these attacks, his wife, Pauline, was killed. But even such a tragic occurrence as this did not deter him from his job, and he continued to use every legal course available to him to pursue his goal of eliminating crime in McNairy County.

His dedication to duty and to his fellow man have made him almost larger than life, and it is only fitting that Tennessee honored him on October 21, 1973. The State of Tennessee declared that day as "Buford Pusser Day in Tennessee," and he was honored at his hometown of Adamsville. Here we also should take note of this man's dedication to upholding the laws of this Nation for the example it sets.

Buford Pusser and Miss Tennessee 1973 Anne Galloway. Pusser and the beauty queen kept steady company for several months. Pusser refused to confirm or deny rumors they planned to be married.

THE LEGACY OF BUFORD PUSSER

Miss Tennessee Anne Galloway and Buford Pusser were the centers of attention during the Pusser Day festivities in October 1973. Standing, from left to right, are Miss Galloway, Pusser, Gene Ferguson, singer Johnny Paycheck, an unidentified fan, and singer George Jones. Sitting is singer Tammy Wynette.

When was the last time you stood up and applauded a movie?

When were you so impressed and involved that you spontaneously cheered?

In theaters across the country, audiences are standing up applauding and cheering "Walking Tall." It is a deeply moving, contemporary film.

"Walking Tall" is based on the true story of a young man who wouldn't surrender to the system... and the girl who always stood by him.

WALKING TALL

CINERAMA RELEASING presents
"WALKING TALL"
Starring
JOE DON BAKER · ELIZABETH HARTMAN
ROSEMARY MURPHY Written by MORT BRISKIN
Music by WALTER SCHARF Executive Producer CHARLES A. PRATT
Produced by MORT BRISKIN Directed by PHIL KARLSON
A BCP Production A service of Cox Broadcasting Corp. In Color

Title song sung by Johnny Mathis On Columbia Records

R RESTRICTED Under 17 requires accompanying Parent or Adult Guardian

FROM CINERAMA RELEASING

Buford Pusser (left) and Joe Don Baker, the actor who portrayed Pusser in the "Walking Tall" movie. Although Pusser never carried a big stick during his law-enforcement days, he often displayed one for movie promotional purposes.

W.R. MORRIS

Buford Pusser prepares for a trip to the "Walking Tall" movie set in Jackson, Tennessee. He frequently visited with the crew, the actors, and the producers during the filming of the motion picture.

This .38-caliber nickel-plated Smith & Wesson pistol was given to Buford Pusser by the firearms company in 1972. Model 19 with a four-inch barrel, it bore the words "Buford Pusser, Sheriff 1964-1970."

Buford Pusser, Bob Bentley, and W.R. Morris during a 1972 autograph session in Tuscumbia, Alabama. Bentley was and still is an avid fan of both Morris and Pusser.

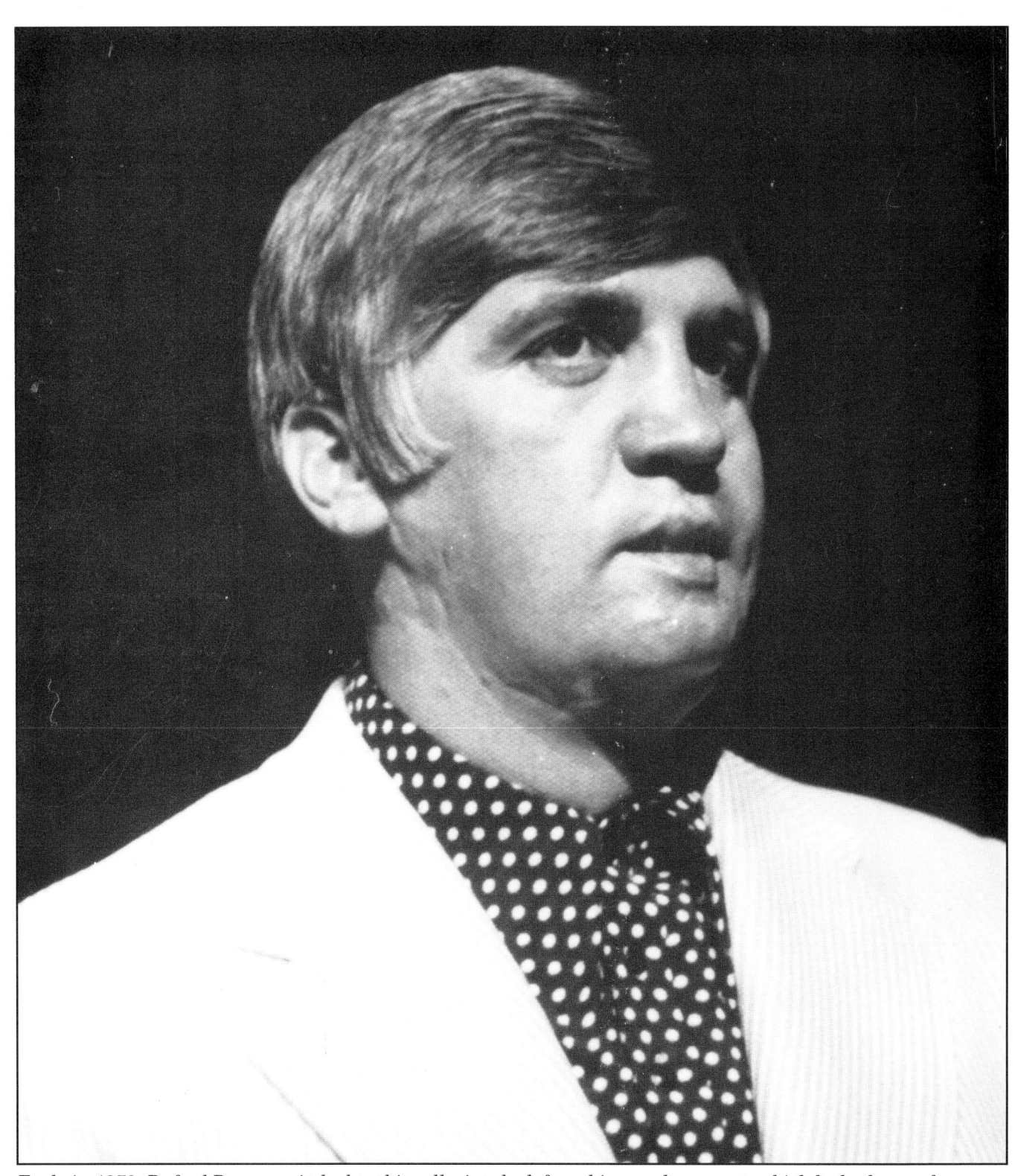

Early in 1972, Buford Pusser switched to this collegiate look from his usual crew cut, which he had worn for many years, including those when he was McNairy County sheriff.

THE LEGACY OF BUFORD PUSSER

Buford Pusser in Little Rock, Arkansas, in 1973.

The Chester County Courthouse in Henderson, Tennessee, was used for most of the courtroom scenes in the "Walking Tall" movies.

Buford Pusser, December 1973, in London, England. He was a special guest of Scotland Yard.

John Wilder, Lieutenant Governor of Tennessee, (left) and W.R. Morris during the "Buford Pusser Day" celebration on October 29, 1973, in Adamsville.

Buford Pusser and his mother, Helen, in April 1974. Buford's dog, "Pug," seems disinterested in the picture-taking activities.

Buford Pusser (right) chats with his close friend Joe Richardson at the Old Home Restaurant and Motel in Adamsville. The restaurant was Pusser's favorite hangout.

The Old Home Restaurant and Motel in Adamsville was not only Buford Pusser's favorite eating place; it also served as his "office." He often met people there to discuss business.

Buford Pusser pauses for a moment in the kitchen of his Adamsville home. Between meals, he often used the table to sort through his mail and conduct other business.

Buford Pusser signs autographs for several youngsters in front of Ray Blanton's campaign headquarters in Chattanooga, Tennessee. From left to right, Bob and Bobby Stanley, Pusser, Susan Madewell, Sheryl Jackson, and Buster Sylar. (Photo by W.C. King, **The Chattanooga Times**)

Gene Crump, owner of the Chevrolet dealership in Tuscumbia, Alabama, hands Buford Pusser the keys to a 1974 Corvette. The legendary sheriff would later perish in the car.

heard of the crime-busting sheriff and his bloodstained career, but most had never seen him. If the famous lawman portrayed himself, fans could see the real Buford Pusser on the screen. Bing Crosby officials jetted Pusser to Hollywood for a screen test, but the results were not made public.

On August 20, 1974, the movie executives held a news

conference at the Holiday Inn Rivermont in Memphis. They announced that Pusser would play himself in a sequel called "Buford." The producers said the film had a $2-million budget and would go into production on September 20, 1974, near Jackson, Tennessee.

Buford Pusser's ego was at an all-time high when he left the press conference. It was difficult for him to envision "an ole country boy" like himself as a movie star.

Alone in his new gray Lincoln Continental, Pusser traveled Highway 57 from Memphis toward McNairy County. He remembered the countless trips he had made down this same highway in an ambulance. Several times during his law-enforcement days, Buford, suffering from stabbings, gunshot wounds, or an automobile accident, lay on a stretcher in an emergency vehicle as it sped from Selmer to the Baptist Hospital in Memphis. Each time he thought it would be his last trip to the Bluff City. Now, ironically – with no thought of his life being in danger – Buford Pusser traveled Highway 57 for the final time.

When he arrived home, he parked the Lincoln inside his two-car

Buford Pusser in New York City on February 19, 1974.

Buford Pusser loved the sleek styling of this 1974 Corvette along with its powerful engine. The car later carried him to his death.

THE LEGACY OF BUFORD PUSSER

Buford Pusser relaxes behind the wheel of his new sports car before departing for another personal appearance date.

Buford Pusser stands beside his Corvette in the parking lot of the Old Home Restaurant and Motel in Adamsville. Pusser died about a week later when the 'Vette crashed into an embankment and burned.
(Photo by Gene Page, **Brandenton Herald**)

THE LEGACY OF BUFORD PUSSER

garage, which was located under the rear of the house and adjacent to his downstairs bedroom. Pusser entered his sleeping quarters and changed from his dark business suit to a pair of blue Bermuda shorts and a navy blue T-shirt.

He planned to mow the grass, then attend the McNairy County Fair in Selmer. Before he could remove the mower from a utility shed, two employees from Maxedon's 66 Service Station delivered Pusser's maroon Corvette to him. He had left the sports car at the station to be tuned up. Abandoning his plans to mow the lawn, Buford decided to test-drive the 'Vette.

When Pusser returned home from road testing the sports car, he learned that his daughter had already left for the fair. He climbed back into the Corvette and headed for Selmer.

The Ferris wheel, festooned with colored lights, hovered above the McNairy County fairgrounds as if it were an object from outer space. As the hands on the clock crawled toward the midnight hour, the crowd thinned. Most of the rides had already shut down. Buford Pusser sauntered toward the front gate, occasionally pausing to sign an autograph.

Earlier in the evening, he had played a few games on the midway and had planned to participate in the Jaycees' dunking barrel event. But his admirers had stolen most of his time by keeping him busy answering questions about his new movie and autographing everything from popcorn bags to fair programs.

Dwana Pusser, Buford's daughter, was also preparing to leave the fair. She had gone there with some friends – Tina Durbin, Shirley Durbin, and Edward Lee Hollingsworth. Dwana spotted her father and ran to him. "Daddy, I'm gonna ride home with Tina. We all came together. You don't care, do you?"

"Course not. See you at the house," Buford grinned.

Pusser strolled across the fairgrounds parking lot toward his car. He stuffed his huge frame into the Corvette, then grabbed one of the two barbecue sandwiches he had left on the seat beside him. He quickly finished the first sandwich and started on the second. He had purchased the food earlier at Coleman's Bar-B-Q in Selmer. After wolfing down the barbecues, Pusser spun from the parking area with the rear wheels of his Corvette throwing gravel through clouds of dust.

Buford Pusser at his Adamsville home in July 1974.

This is a view of the accident scene on U.S. Highway 64 where Buford Pusser died in a fiery car crash. His Corvette skidded 345 feet across the pavement, left the highway, skidded another 200 feet across loose gravel, then slammed into a roadside embankment.

On U.S. 64, Buford saw the taillights of the Chevrolet in which his daughter was riding. He decided to pass, and within seconds, he was out of sight.

Pusser's Corvette hugged the narrow two-lane highway which stretched 13 miles from Selmer to Adamsville. The speedometer needle played with the 100-mile-per-hour mark. The Corvette streaked up a rolling hill and dipped into a flat stretch of highway. At the crest of a slope, the sports car left the road, touched gravel, then returned to the pavement. Seconds later, the car spun counterclockwise and careened sideways out of control. It skidded 345 feet across the pavement, left the highway, skidded another 200 feet across the loose gravel of the parking area in front of a small grocery store, uprooted a stop sign, then slammed into a red clay embankment.

The charred ruins of Buford Pusser's 1974 maroon-colored Corvette. The fiery car crash threw Pusser through the open T-roof. He landed alongside the highway and died from a broken neck.

Tennessee State Trooper Paul Ervin investigated Buford Pusser's fatal car wreck on August 21, 1974. Ironically, 20 years later, Ervin was elected sheriff of McNairy County.

Pusser sailed through the open T-roof of the sports car and landed alongside the highway. The vehicle burst into flames, illuminating Buford Pusser's lifeless body, which was sprawled facedown less than four feet away.

Danny Browder, who lived in a mobile home near the crash site, was watching a late movie on television. He heard what sounded like a low-flying jet. Browder hurried to the window and saw the fire. He rushed out to his car and drove the few hundred feet to the wreck scene. Although Danny Browder had been a classmate of Buford Pusser at Adamsville High School, he failed to recognize the legendary sheriff. Browder returned to his house trailer and telephoned authorities.

As Dwana Pusser and her friends approached the fiery crash, she recognized her father's car. "Stop! Stop! It's Daddy!" Dwana screamed as she leaped from the Chevrolet before it came to a complete halt.

She ran to her father and embraced him, sobbing loudly. "Daddy! Daddy! Talk to me! Please, Daddy, I love you!" she cried, laying her head across his chest.

Shirley Durbin knelt beside Buford's body and placed her hand on his chest. "Buford! Buford! Can you hear me?" Slowly, Mrs. Durbin stood and walked away. She knew that Buford Pusser would never speak again.

Edward Lee Hollingsworth and Dwana Pusser, half carrying, half dragging, moved Buford's body approximately 100 feet from the burning wreckage.

Minutes later, Tennessee State Trooper Paul Ervin and

Dr. Harry Peeler, McNairy County Medical Examiner, arrived. Dr. Peeler, who had patched Pusser up on several other occasions, quickly realized that the legendary lawman would never again need medical aid. Peeler pronounced Buford Pusser dead at the scene – saying he had suffered a broken neck. This date, August 21, 1974, would be forever recorded in the history books.

Countless persons believed that Buford Pusser was murdered in a well-planned automobile wreck. The Tennessee Highway Patrol, however, said Pusser's fatal car crash was accidental. Speed was listed as the contributing factor.

Hundreds of mourners stood outside the Adamsville Church of Christ waiting to view the body of Buford Pusser. Businessmen wearing expensive suits. Uniformed police officers. Farmers in bibbed overalls.

The light blue steel casket containing Pusser's corpse rested at the front of the church on a carriage hidden by a matching ruffled skirt. A wreath of red roses with a green sash that read "Daddy" lay on the coffin. Buford Pusser, lying on the white shirred satin, appeared to have finally found peace. He was dressed in a black suit with red and gray pinstripes, a white shirt, and a blue and red polka-dot tie.

Helen Pusser gazed at her son's body and was haunted by a recent conversation she had heard between him and a reporter. "With the movie having been so big and with all the publicity it generated, where does Buford Pusser picture himself ten years from now? Where will it all end?" the newsman had asked.

Mrs. Pusser remembered that a wide grin creased Buford's face before he answered. "Well. Course, I don't have the slightest idea. My life for the last couple of years has been so hectic that I can't imagine where it will all end."

By early Saturday, August 24, the day of the funeral, more than 3,000 persons had viewed Buford Pusser's corpse. Members of the Pusser family had maintained a round-the-clock vigil at the church since the body had arrived there. It was a custom in West Tennessee for relatives to sit up with the deceased until the funeral.

Shortly before noon, Joe Don Baker and country music stars George Jones and Tammy Wynette arrived in Adamsville. News-

THE LEGACY OF BUFORD PUSSER

Buford Pusser's funeral services were held at the Church of Christ in Adamsville on August 24, 1974. The services were held by the Reverend Russell Gallimore and Bobby Tillman.

men quickly cornered Baker and asked him why he had refused to portray Pusser in the second movie.

"I refused to play Buford in the 'Walking Tall' sequel because the script was lousy, and it is all fiction. It's a bad reflection on Sheriff Pusser," Baker claimed.

The town of Adamsville practically closed down for the funeral. The Old Home Restaurant, one of Buford's favorite hangouts, closed at noon that Friday because it could not accommodate the large crowd in town for the services.

More than 1,000 persons gathered around the red-brick Church of Christ, a small, single-aisle structure with a seating capacity of 300. A sound system was installed outside the sanctuary so that those who were unable to get inside could hear the service.

The funeral observances were conducted by the Reverend Russell Gallimore, former pastor of the United Methodist Church in Adamsville. The clergyman, who was now minister of the Bolivar Methodist Church in Bolivar, Tennessee, had held the religious ceremonies for Buford Pusser Day in 1973. Bobby Tillman, minister of the Adamsville Church of Christ, opened the service with brief remarks about Buford Pusser and his family, all of whom were members of Tillman's congregation.

The choir sang "Rock of Ages," Buford's favorite hymn, followed by "The Last Mile" and "Hold to God's Unchanging Hand."

Buford Pusser's funeral procession passed through the tiny business district en route to the Adamsville Cemetery, which was located on a hill overlooking U.S. 64 at the western edge of town. It was the same route taken seven years ago after Pusser's wife, Pauline, was slain. Buford, fighting to overcome the injuries caused by high-powered bullets that tore away half of his face, had been unable to attend Pauline's funeral.

Among Pusser's casket bearers were Ray Blanton, Glen H. Gray, Shorty Freeland, David Dickey, Gene Crump, Roger Horton, James Woods, and Billy Majors. An army of law-enforcement officers, led by Steve Hood of Shelby County, president of the Fraternal Order of Police, filed past the blue and silver concrete burial vault, each placing a white carnation on the lid. Several admirers of the famous sheriff plucked flowers from the wreaths which surrounded the gravesite to keep as souvenirs.

Buford Hayse Pusser was laid to rest beside his wife in the red McNairy County clay.

★ ★ ★ ★

> August 21, 1994, marked the 20th anniversary of Buford Pusser's death. Still, a steady flow of people continue to visit Adamsville, Tennessee. Guests stroll through the Buford Pusser Museum, snap pictures, ask questions, and seek out those who were personally acquainted with the famous sheriff. The historical heritage of the Buford Pusser legend attracts tourists to Adamsville from all over the United States and many foreign countries.

THE LEGACY OF BUFORD PUSSER

Actor Joe Don Baker, who portrayed Buford Pusser in the "Walking Tall" movie, fights back tears at the legendary sheriff's funeral on August 24, 1974, in Adamsville, Tennessee.

Friends carry Buford Pusser's casket from the Adamsville Church of Christ. Those visible (from left to right) are Gene Crump, Glen H. Gray, Ray Blanton, and James Wood.

Flowers blanket the area near the grave site of Buford Pusser in the Adamsville Cemetery. Floral bouquets were sent from all over the United States.

The footstone at Buford Pusser's grave in the Adamsville Cemetery.

This monument marks the graves of Buford and Pauline Pusser in the Adamsville Cemetery. Buford's parents, Carl and Helen, are buried nearby. The stone was designed by Jimmy K. and Jody Walker of the Walker Monument Works in Bethel Springs, Tennessee.

THE LEGACY OF BUFORD PUSSER

Shortly after Buford Pusser's death, Bing Crosby Productions chose a Swedish-born actor named Bo Svenson to portray the legendary sheriff. With Buford gone, the movie officials decided to name the second film "Walking Tall, Part II." Company press releases spewed the propaganda that this was Buford's own true story. They also claimed that Svenson was similar to Pusser in both personal appearance and character.

Helen Pusser, who called the promotional material "outright lies," had sought a court order to block the release of the project. "Bo Svenson is nothing like Buford. Svenson talks like a foreigner and dresses like a bum in the movie. Buford never wore a pair of blue jeans in his life. Svenson parades around on the screen like a real idiot. When Buford was sheriff, he wore suits and ties. He was a neat dresser. Bo Svenson and the movie are both disgusting," scoffed Mrs. Pusser.

Film critics agreed. "You can rate 'Walking Tall, Part II' PG – in this case standing for pure garbage."

In her lawsuit, Helen Pusser said that the movie should not be marketed because it was "a grossly distorted version of my son's life that damages his true image."

The judge, however, ruled that Buford Pusser had personally given Bing Crosby Productions the exclusive right to film stories about his life. And the contract gave the movie producers the authority to fictionalize the true saga of Buford Pusser.

Unlike the first Pusser film, "Walking Tall, Part II" failed to break any box-office records. When a short-lived television series starring Bo Svenson as Pusser hit the market, the story line was so unbelievable that the series flopped after only six episodes. Brian Dennehy swung the fictionalized Pusser stick in a made-for-television movie called "A Real American Hero." The film acquired some extra Southern flavor when country music star Don Williams sang the theme song. And Dennehy's superb

Bo Svenson.

*Brian Dennehy between scenes during the filming of "A Real American Hero" in Chester County, Tennessee. Dennehy portrayed Buford Pusser in the made-for-television movie. (Photo by Roberta Cude/**Savannah Courier**)*

111

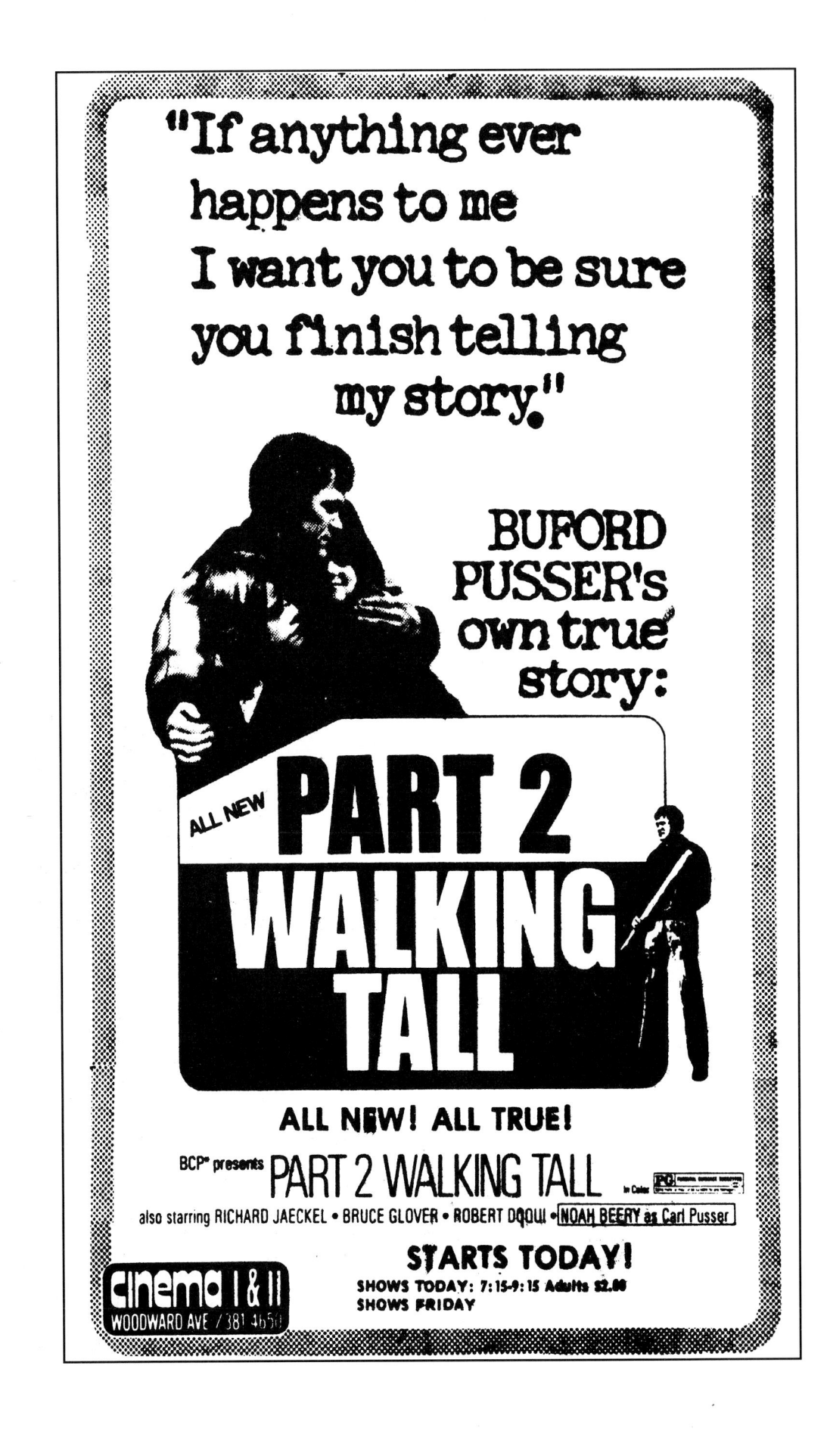

"If anything ever happens to me I want you to be sure you finish telling my story."

BUFORD PUSSER's own true story:

ALL NEW **PART 2 WALKING TALL**

ALL NEW! ALL TRUE!

BCP° presents PART 2 WALKING TALL In Color PG

also starring RICHARD JAECKEL • BRUCE GLOVER • ROBERT DOQUI • NOAH BEERY as Carl Pusser

STARTS TODAY!
SHOWS TODAY: 7:15-9:15 Adults $2.00
SHOWS FRIDAY

cinema I & II
WOODWARD AVE / 381-4650

acting overshadowed the weak script. But officials at Bing Crosby Productions were determined to drain the Buford Pusser film keg dry. They developed a third theatrical release movie, "Final Chapter – Walking Tall." Once again, Bo Svenson played the legendary sheriff. And, once again, the motion picture generated very little interest at the box office.

With the exception of the ill-fated television series, the last film was the worst financial failure of the Pusser productions.

Hollywood script writers could have used Buford Pusser's true experiences to produce a sensational motion picture. Instead, they chose to create fictional episodes and to pad the actual deeds he accomplished.

Wayne Jerrolds, who performed in "A Real American Hero" (a Buford Pusser TV story), was the Mid-South Fiddling Champion from 1958 until 1974. He also wore the state crown, appeared on "Ted Mack's Original Amateur Hour," and played in Grand Ole Opry legend Bill Monroe's band. Jerrolds lives in Savannah, Tennessee.

Buford Pusser went to his grave knowing that Kirksey McCord Nix, Jr., was the chief architect of his wife's murder. After the legendary lawman's death, author W.R. Morris spent months corroborating Nix's role in the New Hope Road ambush.

Only recently, a former deputy United States Marshal said that Nix "was definitely involved" in the slaying of Pauline Pusser. Todd Roseberry, who guarded Nix during his 1991 murder and scam trials in Hattiesburg, Mississippi, believed the gangster had been keeping close tabs on Buford Pusser for years. "Kirksey Nix had one full cardboard box and half of another one with newspaper articles, magazines, and other printed materials about Sheriff Pusser. Some of the articles dated back to the 1967 ambush in McNairy County. His collection looked like a mini Pusser museum," Roseberry said.

"Nix was very talkative. He seemed to enjoy talking to me about

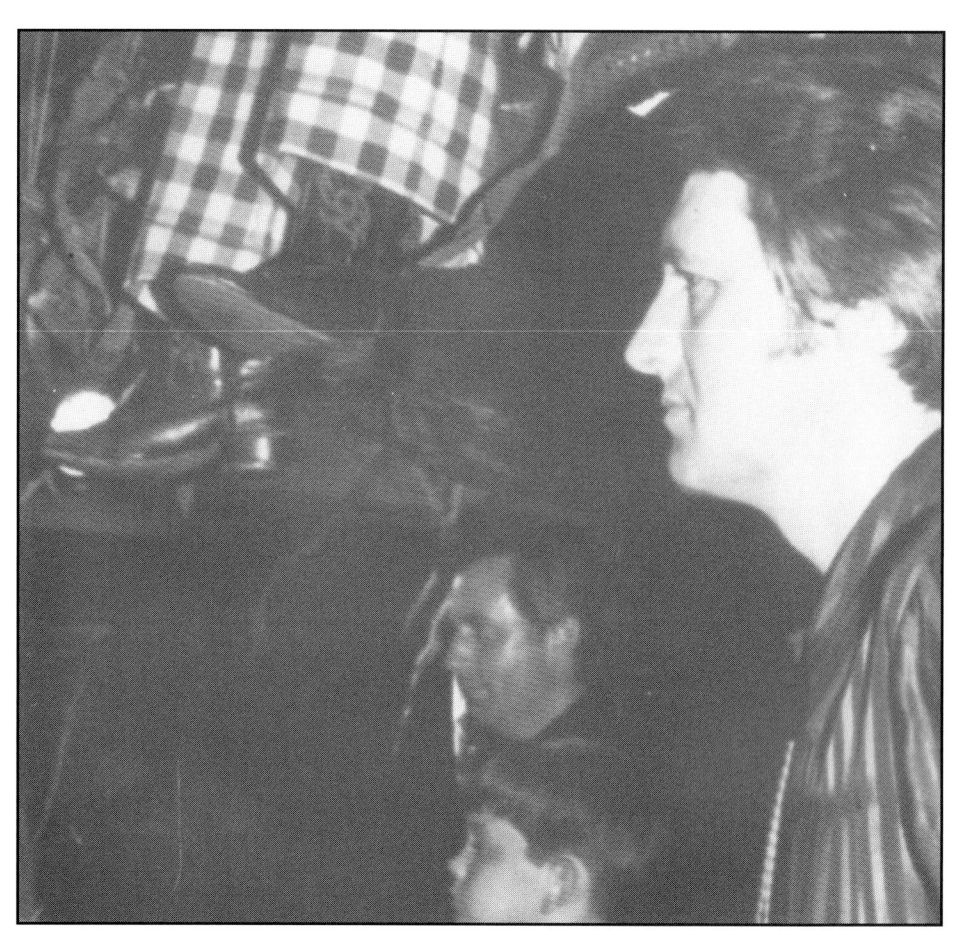

*Wayne Jerrolds (right), banjo player Jimmy Melton, and bassist Bobby Jerrolds on a movie set during the 1978 production of "A Real American Hero" in Chester County, Tennessee. (Photo by Roberta Cude/**Savannah Courier**)*

his many criminal experiences," explained the former federal marshal. "But, when I asked him about Buford Pusser, he clammed up like a mousetrap." Roseberry grew to know Nix well during the two months he watched over the convicted murderer in the Forrest County Jail. "The major thing I learned about Kirksey Nix was that he had a bitter hatred for Buford Pusser. Nix was obsessed with the man. I am convinced beyond a shadow of a doubt that Kirksey McCord Nix, Jr., killed Pauline Pusser," concluded Roseberry.

Buford Pusser was an immaculate dresser. He always wore suits and ties or slacks and sport shirts. His mother said that Pusser had never worn a pair of blue jeans. Neatness was among his top priorities.

TENNESSEE EDITION

THE COMMER

Memphis, Tenn. Thur

The Usual Curious And Souvenir-

Saga Of Bufor

By JOSEPH WEILER
and SHIRLEY DOWNING

Buford Pusser, who gained national fame as the tough bootleg-battling sheriff of McNairy County during the 1960s, was killed early yesterday when his car skidded more than 300 feet and hit an embankment on U.S. 64 near his hometown of Adamsville.

Pusser, 36, was alone in his 1974 maroon Corvette when it left the pavement three miles west of Adamsville, skidded sideways and struck a dirt embankment.

Law enforcement officials said they could not determine how fast the car was traveling at the time of the accident, because there is no way to com-

pute speed from skid marks of a sliding sideways.

The wreck occurred near the where the former sheriff, who had reputation for fast driving, was alm killed about three years ago in a si lar accident which left him hospi ized for about a month.

One law enforcement official s Pusser "drove fast, but safe."

In yesterday's wreck, Pusser's ne was broken and he died instantly, cording to medical reports.

Pusser, who was in Memphis Tu day morning for a press conference announce a sequel to the movie "Wa ing Tall," was driving from a fair Selmer to his home in Adamsville wh the accident occurred. No one was the car with him and no one saw t accident, officials said.

Among the first persons to reach t scene was his daughter, Dwana, and some friends, who were followi at a distance in a second car.

The first person to reach the wre scene was Danny Browder, a form schoolmate of Pusser's at Adamsvi High School, who lives nearby.

"I was watching the late movie wi my daughter when I heard it. I we outside and couldn't see anything so got in my car and found it just up t road.

"I didn't know who it was when I g

Buford Pusser In 1969
With Automatic Rifle

THE LEGACY OF BUFORD PUSSER

AL APPEAL · **TENNESSEE EDITION**

...ing, August 22, 1974

PAGES 47 TO 70

Drawn To Scene Of Wreck

Buford Pusser In 1974
At Tuesday Press Conference
—Staff Photo

Pusser Ends In Wreck

Maxine McDaniel displays a Buford Pusser commemorative knife that was manufactured shortly after the legendary lawman died. Attractively boxed, the knife was designed by Fred Robertson of Finger, Tennessee.

Jason McDaniel of Lexington, Tennessee, holds a sports jacket owned and worn by Buford Pusser. The coat is size 56.

THE LEGACY OF BUFORD PUSSER

Helen Pusser, after Buford's death, spent most of her time promoting the legend of her famous son. She never turned anyone away from Buford Pusser's home in Adamsville. Mrs. Pusser died January 1, 1987.

At the time of his jail stay in Hattiesburg, Nix was serving a life sentence without parole in the Louisiana state prison. He had been convicted of the 1971 Easter Sunday slaying of Frank J. Corso, a wealthy New Orleans grocery store executive. Two of Nix's Dixie Mafia pals – John Fulwood and Peter Frank Mule – were also found guilty of Corso's murder.

On November 11, 1991, an eight-woman, four-man federal jury in Hattiesburg found Kirksey Nix guilty of murder conspiracy and extortion. Three of his cohorts – Mike Gillich, Jr.; John Elbert Ransom; and Sheri LaRa Sharpe – were also convicted. The charges stemmed from the gangland-style murders of Circuit Judge Vincent Sherry and his wife, Margaret, in their Biloxi home on September 14, 1987.

Sherry was a law partner with Pete Halat, who was (at that time) Kirksey Nix's attorney. Halat was handling the gangster's bank funds. When some of the greenbacks disappeared, lawyer Halat could have blamed the thefts on Vincent Sherry. Such accusations would have spelled instant death for the judge. Nix, in jail or out, was a dangerous criminal. He could arrange a hit job with a single telephone call.

Investigators said that Judge Sherry had made a mistake when he became a law partner with Pete Halat. From all indications, Halat was heavily involved in a million-dollar penitentiary scam hatched by Nix. Operating from Angola Prison, the gangster baited homosexuals with advertisements in a national gay magazine. The victims believed that the "young men" in the ads were anxious to join their respondents for homosexual life-styles. But personal problems that only cash could solve always had to be disposed of first.

The money poured in.

Nix and the other scam operators obtained photos of three good-looking young men. They made many copies of the pictures and sent them to each person who answered the ad. Fictitious names were attached to the photographs.

One California victim, Jim Dickey, lost more than $17,000 from mid-September to late October 1988. Shortly after Dickey responded to the ad, he received a phone call from a "teenage boy" who said he had placed the lonely hearts advertisement. The caller identified himself as Eddie Johnson. Actually, "Eddie" was Kirksey Nix.

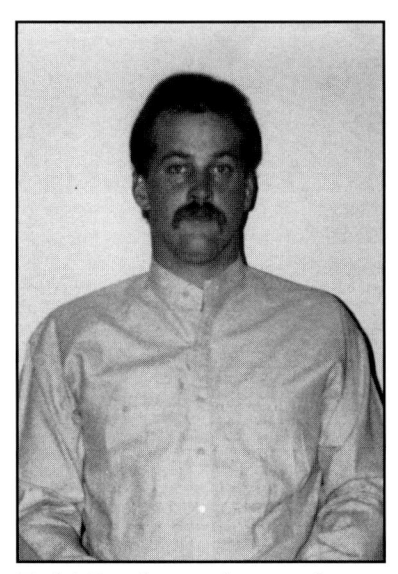

Todd Roseberry, former deputy United States marshal, said he is convinced beyond a doubt that Kirksey Nix, Jr., led the assassination team who murdered Pauline Pusser.

THE LEGACY OF BUFORD PUSSER

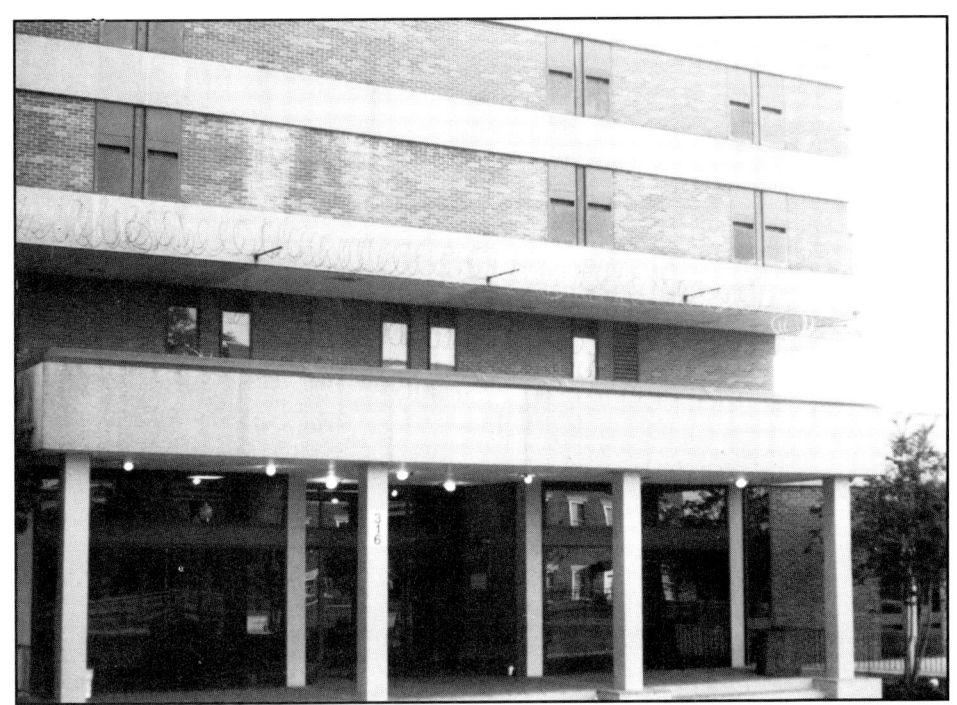

Kirskey Nix, Jr., was housed in the Forrest County Jail in Hattiesburg, Mississippi, before and after his trial for extortion and conspiracy to murder Judge Vincent Sherry and his wife, Margaret. Todd Roseberry, a deputy U.S. marshal at the time, guarded Nix during his two-month stay in Hattiesburg.

Todd Roseberry pauses in front of the William M. Colmer Federal Building in Hattiesburg, Mississippi, where Kirksey McCord Nix, Jr., was found guilty in November 1991 of murder conspiracy and extortion. Three of Nix's pals; Mike Gillich, Jr., John Elbert Ransom, and Sheri LaRa Sharpe; were also convicted.

MEMPHIS, TUESDAY, SEPTEMBER 4, 1990

THE COMMERCIAL APPEAL

Biography of Pusser names Nix in attack

The Associated Press

BATON ROUGE, La. — Dixie Mafia figure Kirksey McCord Nix Jr. led a 1967 ambush that seriously wounded Tennessee Sheriff Buford Pusser and killed his wife, claims Pusser's biographer.

W. R. Morris devotes one chapter of his latest book, *The State Line Mob*, to the McNairy County, Tenn., slaying of Pauline Pusser and the wounding of the sheriff who has been portrayed in movies such as *Walking Tall*.

The book, which relates the activities of a group of gangsters who terrorized the Tennessee-Mississippi border from 1940 to 1970, will be published in October by Rutledge Hill Press of Nashville.

According to Morris, the killing was bankrolled by Carl Douglas 'Towhead' White, a leader of the mob and personal enemy of Pusser's.

Nix, son of an Oklahoma appellate court judge, visited McNairy County several times before the Aug. 12, 1967, attempt on Pusser's life to study the sheriff's movements, Morris said.

Morris said a motel employee reported that Nix and three other Dixie Mafia "hit men" arrived at a hotel near Pusser's home about 11 p.m. on Aug. 11.

Just before dawn, four men parked a late-model black Cadillac behind a church where they could get a view of the highway on which Pusser and his wife were expected to travel that morning, Morris added.

Morris said Pusser told him that he heard the roar of a car beside his vehicle and saw the barrel of a 30-caliber carbine sticking out of the window.

A bullet hit Pauline Pusser in the head, but Pusser was not hit until the Cadillac pulled beside it again. Pusser brought his car to a stop, and the assassins left him for dead, Morris said.

Nix, serving a life sentence at the Louisiana State Penitentiary at Angola, denied any involvement in the ambush during an interview last year.

Nix, 47, has been indicted in connection with prison scams that authorities said bilked homosexuals and others out of hundreds of thousands of dollars.

Nix also denied the existence of a group of gangsters called the Dixie Mafia, saying law enforcement officers in the southeastern United States created a myth to justify their applications for hefty federal law enforcement grants.

The state line mob was "a gang of lawless thugs who had no respect for life or property," Morris said, quoting Sam Ivy, Mississippi's top criminal investigator at the time.

No one was arrested for Mrs. Pusser's murder, Morris said, but after he recovered from his wounds, Pusser spent much of his time tracking down his wife's killers.

"During Buford Pusser's reign as sheriff, he created a larger-than-life image. But while walking tall, he often walked outside of the law," Morris said.

Once, Pusser set fire to beer boxes behind a trouble-plagued county barroom. He also took one of his wife's killers to a remote part of the county, beat him and "shot his trailer full of machinegun bullets from one end to the other," Morris said.

After claiming he wanted a close, intimate relationship, "Eddie" said he had borrowed a car without permission and wrecked it. He explained that he had been arrested and placed in a vocational rehabilitation program.

Over the course of several phone calls, Nix, playing the roles of "Eddie" and a bogus counselor/supervisor named "Ben Dickerson," told Jim Dickey that the authorities would release the young man to him if Dickey would send airline fare. Dickey sent the money and set off a chain of events that would eventually break him.

A string of phony stories followed, including funds needed to pay off the owner of the car "Eddie" had wrecked, a bond to assure his arrival in California, trouble with an incompetent travel agent, and a mugging at the airport. All the problems required money to solve them. Dickey kept the Western Union wires hot.

Finally, Jim Dickey ran out of money and financial sources. Then he became suspicious and contacted a national gay rights lawyer in San Francisco, who put him in touch with a New Orleans attorney. Within a few weeks, Dickey learned he had been duped by a group of con artists living behind the walls of a penitentiary.

Nix used couriers and lawyers outside the prison to send and receive bogus mail, forward phone calls, and handle cash. According to investigators, some of the scam money went through the Pete Halat and Vincent Sherry law offices in Biloxi. Halat, who was later elected mayor of Biloxi, was then Kirksey Nix's attorney.

Nix had purchased a brick veneer home in Jackson County's Gulf Park Estates near Biloxi. Peter Halat was the trustee on a $48,000 loan for the house. Halat's law office managed the Nix account and paid $437 monthly in mortgage installments.

When Nix and his small band of swindlers discovered a half-million dollars missing from the scam fund, they concluded that Vincent Sherry had stolen it. No evidence linking Judge Sherry to the embezzled cash was ever produced. Nix hired Dixie Mafia hit man John Elbert Ransom to kill Sherry. Halat, who was questioned about the murders but never convicted, lost his second bid for the mayor's office.

Margaret Sherry, a purist with impeccable morals, may have been killed with her husband because she was the leading candidate for Biloxi mayor. If elected, Mrs. Sherry's major goal was

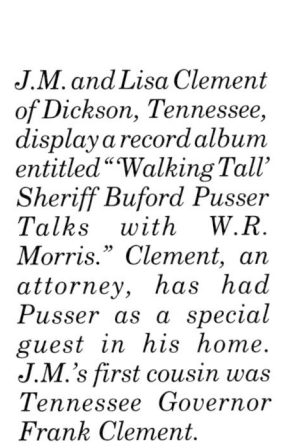

J.M. and Lisa Clement of Dickson, Tennessee, display a record album entitled "'Walking Tall' Sheriff Buford Pusser Talks with W.R. Morris." Clement, an attorney, has had Pusser as a special guest in his home. J.M.'s first cousin was Tennessee Governor Frank Clement.

to rid the city of Mike Gillich, Jr.'s, bawdy striptease joints. Gillich and Nix were close friends.

Nix – with his thinning ash-brown hair, a middle-aged spread, and a prison pallor – was extremely intelligent, cunning, and cold-blooded. Born into a life of privilege and comfort on August 20, 1943, in Eufaula, Oklahoma, he had been entangled with the law ever since he was 19 years old.

His mother, Patricia Kerr, was an attorney. She had divorced Judge Nix when Kirksey was two years old. No matter what the younger Kirksey Nix did, his mom always stood up for him.

The outlaw and his father had much in common. Both were con artists. In 1965, Judge Nix, claiming he was entering into a business deal with movie star John Wayne, sold interest in a development project. Located on 77 acres of land across from the National Cowboy Hall of Fame in Oklahoma City, the enterprise was to include a far-flung amusement complex. The project never materialized. And the investors never saw their greenbacks again.

Also, state investigators launched an ethics violation proceeding against Judge Nix while he was on the bench. He beat the rap.

Kirksey McCord Nix, Jr., will die behind the bleak walls of a Louisiana state prison in the Tunica hills along the Mississippi River. Death may claim him during middle age or linger in the wings until he is an old man. Either way, Kirksey Nix will have paid for his horrible crimes with life's most precious commodity —freedom.

THE LEGACY OF BUFORD PUSSER

Abby Funderburk (left) and Kara Volner, both of Lexington, Tennessee, hold one of Buford Pusser's shirts. The famous sheriff wore a size 18.

*Shannon Funderburk of Lexington, Tennessee, props up a large plywood cutout of Buford Pusser, which was used by the legendary sheriff to promote **The Twelfth of August** book and the "Walking Tall" movie.*

125

A motorist's view of the defunct Shamrock Motel and Restaurant on old U.S. 45 Highway at the Tennessee-Mississippi state line. Time, neglect, and weather have virtually destroyed the Shamrock Motel. Today, it stands in ruins amidst weeds and other debris.

The White Iris Club recently opened again. The new owners have no connection with any of the state-line mob.

Joey Volner, left, examines a gun pouch once owned by Buford Pusser. His brother, Nick Volner, also expresses interest while Shannon Funderburk holds a .32-caliber pistol that the famous sheriff used as a backup weapon.

In 1993, Johnny Nunley, sheriff of Tishomingo County, Mississippi, became the first recipient of the "Buford Pusser Law-Enforcement Officer of the Year" Award. Nunley, 32, waged a tireless war against drugs. His aggressive campaign put large numbers of drug dealers in jail and netted the county more than $100,000 from the sale of confiscated vehicles and other merchandise.

Sheriff Joe Shepard of Gibson County, Tennessee, received the 1994 "Buford Pusser Law-Enforcement Officer of the Year" Award. The sheriff conducted one of the largest drug raids in West Tennessee in 1989. The bust resulted in the confiscation of $26 million in narcotics and cash. Shepard's motto: "I always try to help people instead of hurting them." He has been sheriff since September 1, 1986.

THE LEGACY OF BUFORD PUSSER

Lance Morris stands next to a Tennessee Historical Society marker that denotes where Buford Pusser died in a fiery car crash on August 21, 1974. The accident occurred on U.S. Highway 64 in the Lawton Community near Adamsville.

BUFORD HAYSE PUSSER

On December 12, 1937, Buford Hayse Pusser was born in Finger, Tennessee. In 1962 he became Adamsville's chief of police. He was elected sheriff of McNairy County in 1964. Soon his courageous fight against crime exposed him to much danger and many personal injuries. A movie and a book based on Sheriff Pusser's experiences made him a nationally known hero. He died in an automobile accident here on August 21, 1974.

Jimmy Taylor, deputy sheriff of Alcorn County, Mississippi, with W.R. Morris in front of the Buford Pusser Museum when it was located in the old Adamsville City Hall. Taylor is now sheriff of Alcorn County.

This marker identifies Pusser Street in Adamsville. The home where Buford lived on this street is now a museum.

This sign welcomes visitors to Adamsville, the "Biggest Little Town in Tennessee," and to the Buford Pusser Museum.

THE LEGACY OF BUFORD PUSSER

The Buford Pusser Home and Museum, located at 342 Pusser Street in Adamsville. Countless documents and artifacts once owned by the famous sheriff are housed here. For more information, call 901-632-4080.

This sign in downtown Adamsville points the way to the Buford Pusser Home and Museum located on Pusser Street. The legendary sheriff was living in the house at the time of his death.

Sheriff Paul Barrett of Vicksburg, Mississippi, has a legendary reputation in Warren County for apprehending outlaws and solving crimes. Many of the sheriff's accomplishments are chronicled in a book entitled **Don't Bring Trouble to My County** *by Gerald Smith, Jr. Paul Barrett has a Good Samaritan heart and a Buford Pusser backbone.*

W.R. Morris inspects Buford Pusser artifacts before opening an exhibit at the McNairy County Fair in Selmer in 1986.

THE LEGACY OF BUFORD PUSSER

*Billy Wagoner, owner of the **Community News** in Adamsville and McNairy County historian, sorts through some of his Buford Pusser artifacts. Wagoner also wrote the book **Buford Pusser — The Blood and Thunder Years**.*

Kenny R. Rose (left), consultant with Turner Publishing Company, and Peatie Plunk in 1994. Plunk is the last surviving full-time deputy who worked with Sheriff Buford Pusser.

Country music star Johnny Paycheck (left) and W.R. Morris during a special memorial tribute to Buford Pusser at Hornsby, Tennessee, on August 22, 1987. Grand Ole Opry performer Del Reeves and country artist Allen Frizzell also entertained at the event. (Photo by Cathy Morris)

Ken Oberkfell (left) and W.R. Morris at the Chaffee Christmas Parade. Oberkfell is a former baseball star of the St. Louis Cardinals and the Atlanta Braves. He is a fan of both Morris and Pusser.

THE LEGACY OF BUFORD PUSSER

Norwood Jones stands beside a life-size painting of Buford Pusser. Reed Oliver, Jones's nephew, painted the portrait in 1973. It is on display at the Old County Store in Casey Jones Village in Jackson, Tennessee.

Deep admiration for Buford Pusser spurred Chaffee, Missouri, officials to select W.R. Morris as Grand Marshal of their 1984 Christmas parade. With the author is his son Lance Jay Morris.

W.R. Morris; wife, Cathy; and son Lance view the large crowd who attended the Christmas parade on December 8, 1984, in Chaffee, Missouri.

John Howard Pusser, Buford's 64-year-old brother, was buried in the Adamsville Cemetery. He died on January 24, 1994.

Helen Pusser pins her famous son's sheriff's badge on John Edwards at her Adamsville home. Edwards, who lives in Colonial Heights, Virginia, purchased the gold star from Mrs. Pusser on October 15, 1979.

Larry Price of Selmer, Tennessee, and the "Black Phantom." Price raced this 1966 Chevrolet Caprice against Buford Pusser's cars. Pusser always lost. Price's Chevy has a 427 turbojet engine with 750 horsepower. During the past five years, Larry Price has raised more than $100,000 to benefit West Tennessee children with his annual "Cars for Kids" show in Selmer.

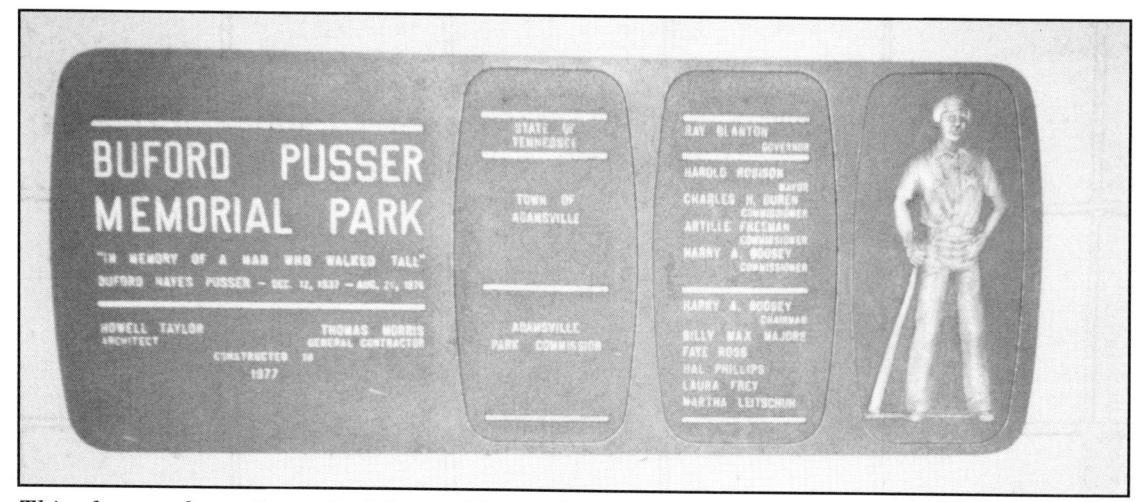

This plaque adorns the wall of the pavilion at the Buford Pusser Memorial Park in Adamsville. Many of the Pusser Day activities are staged at the park each year.

THE LEGACY OF BUFORD PUSSER

Franklin County Sheriff Larry Plott of Russellville, Alabama, is a lawman who also walked tall. During his 18-month undercover investigation, he risked his life and his reputation to smash a deep-rooted criminal empire in north Alabama.

On April 24, 1985, members of the notorious Dawson gang were arrested for drug trafficking, extortion, gambling, racketeering, bootlegging, firearms violations, mail fraud, and counterfeiting. Plott, playing the role of a crooked sheriff, had obtained taped converstations of gang leader Bobby Dawson "paying" Plott to look the other way. Plott's performance as an outlaw sheriff was so convincing that even his wife, his family members, and his friends believed he had been corrupted.

Sheriff Buford Pusser also tangled with some of the Dawsons during his reign in office. They were frequently suspects in various McNairy County crimes. In 1968, Pusser confiscated a truckload of illegal whiskey and beer belonging to Dewitt Dawson.

The Dawsons had long been involved in illegal enterprises in the northern Alabama area. Convicted in the Plott sting were Bobby Dawson; his wife, Lela Mae; sons Duane and Robert; stepdaughter Charlotte Myric; brothers Dewitt and Howard; nephew Billy Ray; and niece Rosa Dawson White. Several other persons in the Dawson ring, including Russellville Police Chief Burns "Buckshot" Saint, were also found guilty of various criminal wrongdoings.

Larry Plott was recently reelected sheriff of Franklin County, Alabama.

Another Tennessee Hero

Dannie Lee Phillips was a Tennessee lawman who applied Buford Pusser grit to wipe out criminal wrongdoings in scenic Anderson County. But, as in Pusser's case, honesty carried a high price tag. Phillips lost his job, his home, and all his worldly possessions and was scorned by many of the citizens.

In 1983, while a deputy under Sheriff Dennis Trotter, Phillips learned that his boss was a crook. He also learned that Johnny Ray Morgan, a fruit-stand peddler with less than a fourth-grade education, was calling the shots at the Anderson County Sheriff's Department. It soon became known among all the deputies that it was risky business to cross Morgan. The outlaw had Trotter, a 33-year law-enforcement veteran who was twice named Tennessee's "Outstanding Sheriff," in his hip pocket.

Morgan recruited Clyde "Soapy" Taylor and Gary Russell into

Dannie Phillips with his cat, "Munchie," in April 1985 at a friend's home in Knoxville, Tennessee.

his illegal enterprises, which included drug trafficking, gambling, prostitution, bootlegging, and bail bond kickbacks. Next, Trotter offered Phillips a "nest egg" in the unlawful business. For smooth sailing, the sheriff needed the chief investigator on his staff in the corrupt fold. Phillips accepted the offer, then contacted the Federal Bureau of Investigation.

During an eight-month undercover probe with the FBI, Phillips, wearing a hidden tape recorder, pretended to be on the take. He discussed drug deals, allowed narcotics from the evidence room at the sheriff's office to be sold by the Trotter gang, and collected his share of the ill-gotten money. The five men often split more than $6,000 weekly. The currency given to Phillips, along with the tapes, was regularly turned over to federal authorities.

Morgan, Taylor, and Russell also operated high-stakes poker and dice games at the Lakefront Tavern. The dive, a large shotgun-styled structure on the banks of Melton Lake between Clinton and Oak Ridge, Tennessee, became the headquarters for illegal activities in Anderson County. Young, attractive women, some barely out of their teens, sold sexual favors to men who could afford to shell out at least 100 dollars for a trip to a back bedroom. The criminal empire was thriving.

Then, on May 21, 1984, the walls collapsed. Sheriff Dennis Trotter, Johnny Ray Morgan, Clyde "Soapy" Taylor, and Gary Russell were arrested by the FBI. All were later convicted of drug trafficking and racketeering. Trotter and Morgan were each sentenced to 15 years in federal prison. Both Taylor and Russell received 20-year terms.

United States District Judge Thomas Hull, who presided at various hearings involving the four men, proclaimed the case "the most open, flagrant corruption of the law I have ever seen."

After Trotter went to jail, Dannie Phillips was named acting sheriff of Anderson County until a special election could be held. He announced his candidacy and sought the Democratic nomination. Apparently, however, the local Democratic Party did not want a sheriff candidate who had an honest track record. Phillips was ignored.

Thomas Van Riper, a close friend of Dennis Trotter, was elected Anderson County sheriff. A retired FBI agent, Van Riper had worked as an investigator for Sheriff Trotter.

Van Riper chose to keep Phillips on his staff. But he immediately demoted Phillips from detective to routine road patrol. It was the first of many maneuvers that would eventually spell doom for the man who had helped slam the prison door shut on Van Riper's old buddy Dennis Trotter.

Next, the new sheriff fired Phillips, claiming he was "irresponsible." Citing Phillips' cocaine use during the FBI investigation, Van Riper also asked the state to revoke Phillips' certification as a police officer. The state complied.

"Of course Dannie used drugs. At times, he had to resort to using drugs to maintain his cover. He could not sit in the corner and sip on a Pepsi if he wanted to maintain his credibility," said his attorney Ron Ridenour.

A former FBI agent said Thomas Van Riper was vindictive and a man of questionable character. On November 17, 1983, Van Riper was refused membership in the Society of Former Special Agents of the Federal Bureau of Investigation in Long Island City, New York. The former federal agent said that Van Riper's application was rejected because he lacked the character required for membership in the FBI's club for retired officers.

A shocking turn of events unfolded next. Many Anderson County citizens turned on Dannie Phillips and labeled him a traitor. "This case, in many respects, is a shocking example of what appears to be happening to a part of America," said Charles Fels, an assistant U.S. attorney. "That any law-abiding citizen could even think about calling Dannie Phillips a traitor is sickening. This young man almost single-handedly exposed the corruption in the Anderson County Sheriff's Office. He risked his life every day as he looked danger in the eye. Without the brave acts of Dannie Phillips, the case never would have come to light," Fels insisted.

Phillips, after losing his house and other personal property, battled money woes by working at various odd jobs. Today, he is still struggling.

Phillips blames most of his troubles on the Federal Bureau of Investigation. "The FBI officials lied to me. They used me until I had nothing else to give. Then they left me in a sinking boat in the middle of the ocean," said Phillips.

The Last Survivor

Peatie Plunk, Buford Pusser's last surviving deputy.

Peatie Plunk is the last surviving deputy sheriff who worked full-time for Buford Pusser. He was the second deputy Pusser placed on the payroll of the McNairy County Sheriff's Department. Jim Moffett, whom Pusser named chief deputy, was the first one hired. Carl Pusser, Buford's father, was employed as jailer and part-time deputy right after young Pusser pinned on the sheriff's badge on September 1, 1964. Carl's primary job was to tend the jail.

Plunk, 32, joined the Buford Pusser force on June 9, 1965. He is a McNairy County native. Today, Peatie Plunk is 61 years old, and he lives in Selmer, Tennessee.

Other full-time deputies on Buford Pusser's staff during his six-year reign as sheriff were Tommy Brown, O.Q. Johnson, Willie Smith, T.W. Burks, and Dave Lipford. The huskily-built Lipford was one of the first full-time black deputy sheriffs in West Tennessee.

A large, framed copy of this Buford Pusser photograph hangs in the corridor of the Adamsville City Hall. Pusser was Adamsville's police chief from early 1962 until mid-1964.